Special Praise for
Parenting the Addicted Teen

"*Parenting the Addicted Teen* is a rich, useful how-to book of the highest order. With clarity, simplicity, depth, and enormous wisdom, Barbara Krovitz-Neren offers a life-changing guidebook parents can use right now to understand their recovering children as they've never understood them before. Barbara redefines healthy parenting as she introduces parents to their recovering children—who they are, what they think, and what they want and need from their parents. Instead of focusing on how to fix the kids, she tells parents to pay attention, listen, and take time to be with their children. This book provides a clear ultimatum for all parents: your kids need you, and here's how you can show up for them. What a fresh, new, enlightened perspective for parents who have been at their wits' end or have given up, or for parents who feel too busy and too burdened by life today to pay attention to their kids. This is a parents' book that puts the focus on the parents, exactly where it needs to be, in a positive, hopeful spirit."

—**Stephanie Brown, PhD, Director, Addiction Institute Outpatient Program, Menlo Park; psychologist in private practice; author of eleven books; researcher, consultant, and lecturer in the field of addiction**

"*Parenting the Addicted Teen* offers a much-needed resource for parents and families struggling with addiction. So often the focus is on getting the addicted loved one into treatment. Parents and families hope that getting their adolescent or young adult into rehab will magically solve the problem. Treatment is an important first step, but in reality the process of healing and recovery is not a straight path. It is one of ups and downs, relapse and renewal, with ongoing stressors that can tax the already-challenged resources of a beleaguered family system. Krovitz-Neren offers a concrete, practical, yet emotionally intelligent model based on her years of experience and research to guide parents through the difficulties of navigating the recovery process in a way that is healing, compassionate, and hopeful. She is finely attuned to the voices and needs of the kids who are desperately fighting for their lives and are so in need of the love and embrace of their families, as well as to the plight of parents who are often frustrated and desperate. An important book for parents *and* professionals!"

—Ann Cusack, PsyD, RN, CADC

"Every parent, not just one of the parents, but *every* parent of a young adult or adolescent struggling with addiction and/or early recovery needs to read this book! Barbara Krovitz-Neren captures the essence of the war-torn family and with great compassion offers a focused path to healing and recovery for the whole family system. She knows her teens and young adults, and she knows their parents. You're no longer out there alone."

—Claudia Black, PhD, MSW, Clinical Architect of the Young Adult Program at the Claudia Black Young Adult Center, The Meadows

"I have been working with youth in recovery from chemical use disorder (CUD) for twenty-one years and have known Barbara Krovitz-Neren for ten years. Throughout those years, parents have reached out and asked if there are any resources I could point them to. Besides the obvious choice of twelve-step fellowships, there are not too many resources for parents of children battling CUD. As their child goes through treatment, parents receive counseling support through the treatment center, but when the child leaves, the support typically ends. Recognizing this, Barbara has done a remarkable job of creating a program to assist parents in recovering in their own right and re-creating a positive family unit once again. Barbara has worked with our students and parents over the years to help in this endeavor. By collecting real-life testimonials from our students, she has been able to synthesize the information in a very meaningful way. She provides useful and specific tools for parents to rebuild the family unit in a positive and healthy manner. At our school, we saw positive growth from the students and received many compliments from the parents who participated in the program.

"I've had the pleasure of copresenting with Barbara at professional conferences as she has endeavored to bring her 5-Step Foundational Parenting Program to a larger audience outside Minnesota. Now, with *Parenting the Addicted Teen,* she can help many more families with her insight and knowledge. By using real-life testimonials from actual adolescents and parents, Barbara has written a thought-provoking parenting manual specifically for parents of young people suffering from CUD. I am grateful not only for the work Barbara has done with our families over the years, but even more importantly, for writing this book, thus providing me an excellent resource to pass along to inquiring parents."

—Michael Durchslag, Director of P.E.A.S.E. Academy, Recovery High School

Parenting the Addicted Teen

Parenting the Addicted Teen

A 5-Step Foundational Program

Barbara Krovitz-Neren

CENTRAL RECOVERY PRESS

LAS VEGAS

Central Recovery Press (CRP) is committed to publishing exceptional materials addressing addiction treatment, recovery, and behavioral healthcare topics.

For more information, visit www.centralrecoverypress.com.

Publisher: Central Recovery Press
          3321 N. Buffalo Drive
          Las Vegas, NV 89129

22 21 20 19 18 17   1 2 3 4 5

Library of Congress Cataloging-in-Publication Data

Names: Krovitz-Neren, Barbara, author.
Title: Parenting the addicted teen : a 5-step foundational program / Barbara
    Krovitz-Neren.
Description: Las Vegas, NV : Central Recovery Press, [2017] | Includes
    bibliographical references.
Identifiers: LCCN 2017012380 (print) | LCCN 2017020862 (ebook) | ISBN
    9781942094449 (ebook) | ISBN 9781942094432 (pbk. : alk. paper)
Subjects: LCSH: Teenagers--Drug use. | Drug addicts. | Child rearing. |
    Parents of drug addicts.
Classification: LCC HV5824.Y68 (ebook) | LCC HV5824.Y68 K76 2017 (print) |
    DDC 649/.152--dc23
LC record available at https://lccn.loc.gov/2017012380

Photo of Barbara Krovitz-Neren by Alice K. Egan.

Cover design, interior design, and layout by Deb Tremper, Six Penny Graphics.

I dedicate this book to all the kids I've
worked with throughout my career.
You've shared with me your heartfelt wisdom
and helped me understand what kids
of all ages need from their parents.

Table of Contents

Foreword

I first met Barbara when I founded my first center for children from difficult—mostly alcoholic—families. While I was putting together my ideas for a pilot program, one name kept coming up. That name was Barbara Krovitz-Neren. We had few resources and many dreams. I approached her and shared my dreams. Our dreams matched. We both had stars in our eyes and realism in our hearts. Barbara came to work with me, and we made many of those dreams come true.

We were given a building in Minneapolis, and the children's program began. She was my first employee. Her love of children and her concern for their welfare bubbled out of her. She was successful with them from day one. Family love and family blending have been her life's work. Out of her personal and professional skill and devotion has come a body of work designed to help others walk down a path of being there for children and parents.

Connection in family systems is hard, and often difficult to navigate. We must forge new ways of thinking as we shift from being the one who is in charge to the one who is often tired and questioning his or her "in charge" role. Are we doing it right? Can I be a better person? There are countless questions we ask of ourselves as we do the best we can. It only gets harder as the people around us grow and change and have their input on how we are doing. Life gets complicated, and we carry on as people and as parents. In my travels across the world and its many cultures, I have found a universal, basic need to love and to nurture, regardless of how well we are doing.

Barbara's research is a prime example of what I believe. Sometimes we have research-based evidence on a subject, and sometimes we have evidence-based research. She has both.

Barbara has talked the talk, but more importantly, she has walked the walk. She has worked with many children, teenagers, young adults, and their parents. She has done her homework, and now she shares her findings in the book before you.

Life presents stress and trauma for many teenagers whose parents never "had the chance" or "took the chance" to recover from their pain before starting families of their own. In that way, the illness perpetuates itself from generation to generation. This book will guide both parents and their children in finding recovery.

Barbara offers theories and lessons for how to break the cycle of family pain, especially with regard to parenting. Her book will serve as a guide for individuals, families, and professionals to create a structure and a foundation upon which to build new family systems and leave a legacy of health and recovery. It's never too late for parents to turn away from stress and addiction with their kids of all ages and solidify their foundation in order to parent with strength and commitment. It's never too late to have a happy childhood!

Sharon Wegscheider-Cruse,
renowned family therapist, founding chairperson of the
National Association for Children of Alcoholics,
author of numerous books including *Another Chance:
Hope and Health for the Alcoholic Family* and *Learning
to Love Yourself: Finding Your Self-Worth*

Preface

This book represents my life's work, professionally and personally. For the past forty years, I have been a parent just like you. From becoming a single parent when my daughter was just two years old to remarrying and blending a family of four children, I have faced many challenges on my path. At times, my heart ached just like yours. I had a dream of being *that* parent—the one who is totally connected to her children and who creates wonderful, meaningful family experiences and makes the most of daily life. Sometimes I had to deal with the dark side of life without letting it consume me. There were the fear of the unknown, unpredictable health issues in the family, addiction challenges of loved ones, aging parents, and a career that challenged my time commitment to my family.

The question I asked myself over and over was, "How can I be more present in my interactions with my children and not focus so much on the stress and unpredictability of life's challenges?" So often I would think, *If only these problems weren't on my path, I could be a better parent.*

I was blessed with a positive spirit that helped me to continuously regroup so I could show up each day for my children as much as possible. Sometimes, I was able to be present. Other times, I obsessed over an issue. When I was trapped in my thinking, I couldn't be completely available. Stress seized me, and I wasn't in charge. When stress took over, I became intolerant, impatient, judgmental, and unable to carve out time to connect with my children. For me, the central challenge was to embrace everything on my path, acknowledge it, see it, and not let it take me away from the present moment.

Then one day I had an "aha" moment. I saw that I could be in charge of how I thought, of how I reacted, and of the decisions I made. I realized that challenges don't have to control me and take away my spirit. This clarity helped me see my daughter and stepchildren in a totally different light. When I could be present in body, mind, and spirit and show up to accept others as they were in the moment and not how I wished they would be, I was able to connect with them no matter what was going on in my personal life.

The truth is, my main goal was to be the best parent I could be to support my children throughout their adolescence and young adult life. I focused on creating a family that would be connected forever. I believe all parents try their best to be good parents based on their own life experiences. No parent wakes up in the morning and consciously decides to try to harm their children's self-esteem and spirit.

What I know from my own life and from the experiences with all the children I have worked with throughout my career is the distance children feel from their parents, a distance that in turn translates into a feeling of responsibility for having caused their parents to "check out." Children may think, *What's wrong with me that my parents don't pay attention to me?*

Throughout my career, the voices of children, teenagers, and young adults have shaped my approach to helping parents regain their role of being in charge of their families. I have worked with thousands of children of alcoholics, recovering teenagers, and recovering young adults. Over the past three years I have polled some 300 teenagers and young adults, collecting their insights and thoughts on parenting. These insights have inspired me to present their collective perspective to you. Their wisdom has played an important part in the creation of this book and of the 5-Step Foundational Parenting Program that enables parents to regain positive energy in their families.

As I have witnessed firsthand, many parents simply do not have the necessary foundation to step into their parenting roles and to reorganize family dynamics so that they are in charge of their children and circumstances. Stress, divorce, addiction, and mental health challenges often take center stage, and then everything revolves around the "issue," which results in the parents' absence. Parents may show up physically, but they are emotionally ungrounded and unavailable to their children. Children pay a high price for that absence. Truthfully, many of us become so absorbed in life's difficulties that we give our sense of self over to stress and lose our grounding, our true foundation.

In this book I will teach you how to take back your power, how to detach from the addiction and mental health challenges in your family, how to turn around, and how to greet your children in new ways that will help you and them grow and flourish with the support of a strong foundation.

We are all able to face up to life's stressors by recognizing the habits that keep us stuck in the same old routine. Sometimes we get headstrong and decide that everyone else is wrong and we are right. Often, we just give up because our challenges feel too difficult and overwhelming.

In my journey, I learned how to rise and face up to these challenges through a thirty-year meditation practice, the twelve-step fellowships, workshops, personal therapeutic work, and my many professional experiences.

I have worked with thousands of children, teenagers, and young adults for over thirty-five years. I have also worked with thousands of parents through school systems, community programs, prevention programs, training workshops, treatment centers, and sober-living homes to help them create a strong foundation upon which they can build, or rebuild, their families. These children, teenagers, young adults, and parents have also been my teachers. They have shared their hearts and souls with me. Every individual is affected in a unique way by their own addiction, the addiction of a loved one, or the influence of someone with a mental health challenge. Many parents have had to deal with hopelessness, sadness, anger, and profound losses. Yet, with help, they have each survived and have risen to a new level of health and joy as a result of applying the 5-Step Foundational Parenting strategies.

Your present to your child is to *be* present—easily said, difficult to do. We are all caught up in habits of familiarity, and in order to change, we first need to understand how our actions affect those we love the most: our children and our partners. Children of all ages need their parents to be present. To be present means to join them where they are in the moment you are with them—without judging them, without hurting them, and without shaming them. They need you to understand who they are and what they need, and to know that they have your unconditional love on their journey.

You might think this is obvious, but what I have learned over the years is that many teenagers and young adults feel lonely, unloved, and distanced from their parents. They need their parents even more when life's heartaches pull their parents away from them, emotionally and/or physically. They clearly know what is missing, and what they need from you.

This book will help you take back your role as a parent and teach you what you can do to strengthen your relationships and your children's core. You *can* make a difference at any stage. It is never too late to begin!

Acknowledgments

I wouldn't be where I am today without the kids I've worked with through the years. They openly shared their broken hearts and wisdom to help me understand what they needed. I also want to thank all the parents who trusted me to help them reclaim themselves and take back their power.

I couldn't have written this book without the unconditional support of my dear husband and best friend. He believed in my journey and always found time to listen to my ideas. Also, I am truly thankful to my sister, a therapist and dear soul. She read and reread parts of this book, helping me when I was stuck.

My children continue to inspire me to see, hear, listen, and love with all my heart. I owe a debt of gratitude to all my friends for their support and friendship. A special thank you goes to Central Recovery Press for believing in my work and helping me make this book available to all parents touched by addiction.

Introduction

The lack of support for parents in the addiction and mental health field during and, even more so, after treatment astounds me. Parents play an essential role in helping sustain a teen's recovery. So, first, I want to acknowledge your pain and the lack of adequate instruction you have available to you. I also want you to know that you *do* play a key role in your child's recovery, a role you can only fill by learning how to step back so that your child can step forward.

When teenagers and young adults are in active addiction, their struggle negatively shifts the family system by pulling the parents into a sticky web of despair. The parents often lose themselves to the burden of not knowing what to do or how to best support their children or themselves. Everyone involved becomes miserable, scared, disgusted, disoriented, and sad. The dreams parents had for their children are lost to addiction, and the reality of "what is" becomes difficult to grasp.

When I lead weekend retreats for parents of young adults in recovery and when I work with parents of teens in recovery, many amazing "aha" moments take place. Participating in the 5-Step Foundational Parenting seminars and workshops helps parents feel supported and gives them the confidence to disentangle themselves from the web of drama created by addiction. They find a renewed sense of freedom and go on to have a healthier relationship with their children. This 5-Step program doesn't negate the need for the twelve-step fellowships—to the contrary, it complements the Twelve Steps.

As you learn about the 5 Steps of Foundational Parenting throughout this book, you will have a chance to reflect on your own experience by taking the action steps presented in each chapter. Here is a roadmap of what you'll find in the rest of this book:

- Thought-provoking glimpses into what teenagers and young adults most want their parents to know, in their own words.
- An explanation of how your family has shifted to accommodate the unwanted behaviors in your teen and how you likely became stuck in habits of unhealthy parenting.
- The 5 Steps of Foundational Parenting that will guide you in disengaging from the addiction and help you regain your parenting power in a healthy way.
- A series of questions to help you put your journey into perspective.
- A plan for putting the 5-Step process to work for you along with a Thirty-Five Day Challenge to get you motivated.
- Suggestions for developing new responses to common dilemmas you may experience with your newly sober child.
- Tips on how to recognize when you fall into old parenting patterns that interfere with your child's recovery.
- Instructions for developing your own personal parenting relapse plan.
- An opportunity to clarify your family values and boundaries.
- Parenting insights that summarize the main ideas at the end of each chapter for your easy reference.

This book will challenge you to reclaim your parenting power while giving you the tools you need to do just that. The parents I know who have implemented these steps have experienced remarkable breakthroughs and discoveries, and these repeated positive outcomes have motivated me to continue helping other parents learn these important tools. The most complex families—hurting parents who are struggling with hopelessness and despair from dealing with their child's addiction—have found strength in these strategies. The 5 Steps have helped them reestablish a healthier family for everyone—yes, even in the face of relapse or another treatment.

You will appreciate the great wisdom shared by the teenagers and young adults in this book. These children, with their aching hearts, never intended to hurt their parents or destroy their families. The same is true of your child. Your child needs you and feels remorse for the pain and suffering he or she has caused. As one of them poignantly stated: "I wish you knew how sorry I am for the pain, worry, fear, and financial hardship I have caused. I am sincere in my desire to be sober and make things right. I am doing the best I can."

By the end of this book you will understand the steps you can take to disentangle yourself and your family from the web of addiction and how to avoid absorbing your child's negative thoughts, feelings, behaviors, and problems. I invite you to come on this journey with me, to learn how to turn hopelessness into hope, and to experience success after so much defeat. It is time for greater stability, increased joy, and a return to your true self.

Chapter One

Paying Attention to What Your Child Needs

"Grown-ups never understand anything for themselves, and it's exhausting to provide explanations over and over again."
—Antoine de Saint-Exupéry, *The Little Prince*

When we listen carefully, as I have done with thousands of children, we realize that they instinctively know what they need from their parents, and what can help their families heal. I am taking this unique opportunity to act as a spokesperson and to share with you the wisdom and insights from hundreds of teenagers—insights that arise from the core of their being—and relay to you in clear terms what it is that they need from you, their parents.

"If I was a parent, I would listen to my kids and love them.
I would let my kids feel their own pain, acknowledge
what they feel, and understand it from my heart."
—Sarene, age eighteen

This chapter sets the stage for the work ahead by giving you a thought-provoking glimpse into what teenagers want their parents to know. These comments offer profound insight into the parental needs of children of all ages.

Parents feel wounded when their children withdraw from them emotionally and physically, and especially when their children struggle with addiction issues. Children feel wounded when their parents' time is consumed with focusing on the issues. Many parents might be in the same room with their child, but mentally they are consumed with stressful and anxious thoughts regarding their child, their job, or their life. Has this happened to you? Does your child give you the silent treatment, groan, smirk, or even scream at you? Has your child accused you of never understanding them? Instead of simply listening without reaction, many parents personalize their child's responses, and feel sad and upset.

Many parents tell me that living with the addiction challenges of a loved one in their family is like living in a war zone. They never know what's going to happen next and feel disempowered and defeated by fear and uncertainty. Children feel the same way under these circumstances, never knowing who will crack under the pressure first. They also feel defeated. Parents want it to be different, their children want it to be different, but no one knows where to begin—until now.

Some Background on the Children Surveyed

Let me give you some background on the lives of the teenagers and young adults you will hear from throughout this book. These individuals are either just out of treatment and going to a recovery high school, or in a sober-living situation for young adults after treatment for additional support with sobriety. Many of them have been through treatment anywhere from one to nine times. Drugs of choice range from alcohol to marijuana to street drugs, prescription drugs, designer drugs, opiates, and heroin. Many of them have been bullied in grade school, middle school, and high school. Quite a few of them have been sexually or physically abused. Developmentally, many experience delays socially, emotionally, intellectually, and spiritually.

Through the years, I have worked directly and indirectly with thousands of adolescents and young adults all over the country. Their stories are heartfelt and telling. Many are children of addicts, many are in recovery, and many have co-occurring mental health challenges. Most of them don't know how to step out from active addiction and remain sober. They all share the following feelings in common: (1) remorse for what they have done to their families; (2) loneliness, sadness, rage, fear, and shame; and (3) love for their parents.

These children come from all sorts of backgrounds: loving families, divorced families, single-parent families, abusive families, addicted families, foster families, wealthy families, middle-income families, and impoverished families. Several were raised by nannies because their parents were too busy with other things to give their children personal care and attention.

Many of these children have mental health challenges that went untreated or were unsuccessfully treated. These include depression, anxiety, severe mood disorders, and learning disabilities. Many of these children mask untreated mental health issues with addiction to ease their pain. Most of the teenagers and young adults have dual diagnoses of chemical dependency with coexisting mental health challenges.

Different Children, Similar Messages

No matter where these children come from, no matter their substances of choice, and no matter their ages, the message to their parents is the same:

- *Be present with me, physically and mentally.*

- *Build a relationship with me.*
- *Console me if I am having a problem.*
- *Do absolutely everything to stay together and not get divorced.*
- *Don't let your mental health problems wreck your family's life.*
- *Don't try to buy me off with things or trips.*
- *Attend a twelve-step program to better understand me.*
- *Give me more attention.*
- *Have family dinners and get to know me.*
- *Help me know I'm not a bad person.*
- *Hug me once in a while.*
- *Keep addictive substances away from me.*
- *Learn how to remain calm when bad things happen.*
- *Let me mess up until I'm ready to change.*
- *Listen to my point of view.*
- *Make sure I know that I can tell you anything without judgment.*
- *Make sure the rules in our family are enforced no matter how moody you feel.*
- *NEVER abuse me, physically, mentally, or emotionally.*
- *NEVER hurt or get violent with me.*
- *NEVER scream or swear at me.*
- *Don't push your burdens on me.*
- *Separate your work from your family time with me.*
- *Show interest in my life at home and school.*
- *Show me that you love me.*
- *Stop complaining about everything I do wrong.*
- *Take time to learn how I think and feel.*
- *Treat everyone in our family the same way.*
- *Try to be positive about life.*

Review this list and think about whether or not your child has expressed similar sentiments, through either their words or their actions. This feedback clearly explains what children need from their parents. Think about the list personally. How many items can you relate to in your relationship with your child? How many items do you need to work on? When your child was using, were you able to fulfill his or her needs and remain in charge? How about now? Becoming conscious of these needs is the first step in approaching your parenting with renewed hope and power.

Seven Key Messages Children Want Their Parents to Know

The messages listed above can be grouped into the following seven themes, which reflect my interpretation of the survey responses and what I've been told by children over the years. Take a look at these statements and take note of the ones you can do easily now. When your child was in the throes of addiction, how did the ones you relate to change? Think about which messages you want to work on in your current parent-child relationship:

1. I want you to understand and value me.
2. I want you to create time for me in your day.
3. I want you to be in charge of our family and not let my moods influence you.
4. I don't want to take care of you emotionally. If I am moody, mad, or upset, please don't take it personally.
5. I want you to protect me and make sure my needs are taken care of.
6. I want you to teach me to be independent and responsible.
7. I want you to love me and show me that you care with actions, not just words.

Expressing Awareness and Remorse

The majority of teenagers in recovery expressed remorse for the painful challenges they put their parents through. The majority of them were clear on how the addiction affected their relationship with their parents. Nevertheless, parents often don't realize that their children really do feel remorse for what they put them through with all of the lies, moodiness, drama, and emotional distance. Many of the parents I meet with have difficulty believing their children feel remorse for their actions while in active addiction. By not being conscious of their child's remorse, these parents still just want to scream at their children for ruining their family and making everyone miserable.

Parents need to learn to step back from the need to blame and begin to forgive. They need to learn to detach from the effects of addiction by moving away from it to rebuild their foundation. It will take time to rebuild trust with the recovering child, but it starts with an awareness that the child, newly in recovery, has a need to be supported and is, in fact, in recovery for the purpose of moving forward and growing beyond the negative effects.

Here is how some of these young adults and adolescents answered the question "How has addiction affected your relationship with your parents?"

- *They lost trust in me, and I'm not sure when it will ever come back.*
- *My addiction further distanced our relationship.*
- *I've lost time with my parents, but I've gotten closer with them. I rely on them too much now. I am a little embarrassed, but also appreciative.*
- *My mother gave up any expectations of me long ago. Our relationship is better now that I have less contact with her.*
- *When I was depressed, I totally shut down and blocked my parents out, which only caused them to try harder.*
- *My addiction caused my mom to be sad all the time.*
- *My addiction was like a heavy fence around me, keeping out my parents.*
- *We had so much drama and endless arguments.*
- *I hurt their feelings all the time.*
- *It pushed us apart, and we had no family time.*
- *We had no understanding of each other because I was so headstrong.*
- *My addiction has strained our relationship.*

- *My mom was unaware of my use. It made me withdraw and prevented an honest, authentic relationship.*

Has your child expressed remorse or asked for forgiveness for his or her behavior while under the influence of addiction? If so, did you feel as if he or she was just trying to manipulate you into forgetting the damage caused over the past years? Are you stuck here? Whether or not your child has verbally expressed remorse, can you begin to let go of your anger, sadness, and distrust—or do you feel you need more time to really let go and see your child in a new light? Think about whether or not you are holding on to leftover feelings. These "leftovers" often interfere with being in the present moment and with family recovery in general. Old feelings that keep surfacing often make parents highly reactive, even when their children are doing well.

The Struggle of Staying Sober

You can play an important role in your child's sobriety when you learn to step back and be a parent who refuses to give in to the obsession that often accompanies addiction. A child's addiction tends to bring out the worst in parents, who feel frustrated, angry, and powerless, and who are often stuck in denial and fear. These emotions consume the parents' energy and take them away from the rest of the family. Recovery is the time for parents to regroup and refocus on the children. Here is what teenagers want their parents to understand while they are making the effort to remain sober:

- *Please understand how fragile I am in early recovery.*
- *I am headstrong and have a difficult time with another point of view. Please keep trying and don't give up on me.*
- *I get depressed easily.*
- *I am my own person, not who you want me to be.*
- *I can't do recovery alone; I need you to love me and support me.*
- *I want you there for me.*

- *I love you even though I don't always show it.*
- *You need to understand I am a better person now.*
- *My spirit can be easily shattered.*
- *I love you and never wanted to hurt you with my using.*
- *Please show me that you love me.*

Can you join your child today in his or her recovery, while understanding that you don't need your child to be sober for you to function as a strong, take-charge parent? Long-lasting recovery takes a good deal of time, and each day is important. Your child needs you to validate the daily process he or she is going through. Your child will be growing and learning new strategies to deal with his or her emotional ups and downs. This takes place in each child's own time and at each child's own pace. Do you allow for this process, or do you try to nudge your child along?

For recovery to be lasting, parents need to realize that it is up to their children to turn to their recovery support system and do the work required. During this process, a parent's job is to listen and be nonreactive. Start listening now so that you come to understand your child's point of view without trying to change it, even if you disagree. Your role is to respect your child's journey, even if it is in baby steps. Unfortunately, when children share their struggles and difficult emotions with their parents, the parents tend to "freak out," thinking the child will start using again, and become frightened and reactive. In truth, many children just need their parents to listen to them and then to validate that they have been heard, not judged. Can you hear your child and accept what he or she tells you as his or her personal truth, or do you try to discourage negative feelings in the hopes that he or she "can be happy"?

Many of the teenagers I've spoken with have expressed feeling lonely around their parents because they don't feel heard by them. Their parents just want everything to be okay and keep trying to make them feel happy, rather than embracing them wherever they happen to be with their thoughts and emotions in the present moment.

From a Child's Perspective

Children can be incredibly expressive when given the chance. However, many children do not have a healthy outlet through which to express themselves. Often, they turn to addictive substances to deal with their pent-up emotions, or they become depressed and hopeless. Many teenagers keep journals to write about their thoughts and emotions. Some express themselves through poetry to expose what they are thinking or feeling in a safe, creative way.

Below is a thought-provoking poem that beautifully summarizes what teenagers and young adults need from their parents. Its author attended a recovery high school and submitted this poem to the school's literary magazine. It is reprinted here with permission.[1]

Because I am your kid you let me have my space
Because I am your kid you don't push me away
Just because we fight, does it mean I don't want you in my life?
No.
It means I need you in my life
When I say I want to run away, it doesn't mean I really do
It's just to show you I want my way
Sometimes I want to get away, but I know I can't because I'm here to stay
Sometimes I think I hate you but in actuality it's never true.
Because I am your kid let me be free
Listen to what I have to say, always believe in me
And I'll always be here to stay.
Until I get older of course

---

1 Published in the P.E.A.S.E. Academy High School literary magazine, 2012. Reprinted with permission.

I'll never be far enough so that you miss me and realize sometimes my way
    was the right way.
Although it may not always be the right way,
Sometimes it is.
So listen,
Because I am your kid.

Your Children Want You on Their Side

Teenagers can get in the habit of playing games with their parents by acting like they don't care and seeming unresponsive to their parents' conversations. In truth, almost all of the teenagers surveyed clearly want their parents on their side. Children may act out, show intolerance of you, and express disdain when you put expectations on them, but they truly do want you to be in charge and to take back your power as a parent.

Listening to your children, greeting them where they currently are, taking back your power, and reestablishing your family are the essence of what you're learning from this book. As you experiment with the 5 Steps of Foundational Parenting starting in Chapter 3, be aware that "walking on eggshells"—avoiding saying or doing certain things because you are afraid of how your child will react to you—will eventually have to cease. You will have to face all the dilemmas head-on and learn how to clarify your family values, boundaries, and expectations.

"Re-trusting" your child is a lengthy process, and it's important to understand that it will take time. Trust the moment, from one to the next. The 5 Steps will teach you strategies for how not to absorb your child's thoughts, feelings, moods, or problems, and how to respond to his or her thoughts and feelings from a place of support, understanding, and nonattachment. This means you will learn to disengage from the powerful magnet of addiction and not be pulled back in by its force.

When you clarify your family values, boundaries, and expectations, you will have a clearer idea of how you want your family to operate and what you won't tolerate—no matter how old your children are. You will learn how to join your children where they are and better understand their thoughts, feelings, and challenges. You will learn how to listen without judgment to your child's messages, stories, and feelings. You will also have the opportunity to regain and restore yourself as you work the 5 Steps.

As you begin this journey of rebuilding your foundation, keep in mind what children need and want their parents to know, but always remember that your journey belongs to you. As you practice, you will soon realize that you *can* restructure your family and reestablish your role as a parent who is present, caring, and supportive, despite all the difficulties and challenges you are facing.

Parenting Insights

- Parents feel wounded when their children withdraw from them emotionally and physically, and especially when those children also struggle with addiction issues. Children feel wounded when their parents' time becomes consumed with focusing on the issues.
- The majority of the teenagers and young adults surveyed express remorse for the painful challenges they put their parents through. Parents often don't realize or believe that their children really do feel remorse.
- The majority of teenagers and young adults are clear about how the addiction has affected their relationship with their parents.
- Parents need to learn to step back from the need to blame and begin to forgive. They need to learn to detach from the effects of addiction and begin to rebuild their foundation.
- Children need their parents to validate the daily process they are going through. Young people in recovery will grow and learn new strategies to deal with their emotional ups and

downs. This takes place in each individual child's own time and at each child's own pace.

- Teenagers and young adults want their parents to listen to what's on their minds and to validate what they've heard them say without judgment.
- Parents can play an important role in a child's recovery when they learn to step back and be parents who refuse to give in to the obsession that often accompanies addiction.
- Teenagers and young adults may act out, show intolerance, and express disdain when parents put expectations on them, but they do want their parents to be in charge and to take back their power as parents.

Chapter Two

Looking at What Interferes with Healthy Parenting

Healthy parenting is crucial for a child's continued recovery. A healthy parenting approach does not allow for a child's moods or actions to evoke reactions that escalate into a destructive situation. The addiction or threat of a relapse is no longer permitted to rule the home, depleting the parents' energy and power. When parents are clear about their values and expectations and adhere to them, children can push and test the limits, but in the face of healthy parenting they won't succeed in coercing their parents into bending the rules. In this way, children know that parents "mean what they say and say what they mean."

This chapter will identify what interferes with successful parenting—not just of your child with addiction, but of all of your children. You will learn how parents give away their power to their chemically dependent child. You will learn how addiction yanks parents away emotionally from the rest of the family, including their spouse and other children.

You will begin to identify the triggers that keep you trapped and absorbed in your addicted child's life. You will also learn about some of the mistakes parents have shared with me that they made when their children first came home from treatment or home for a visit, so that you can learn from them and hopefully avoid them.

Once you recognize the traps, you will be able to catch yourself when you slip back into old behaviors or situations. These triggers prevent well-intentioned parents from detaching from the issue and keep them from taking charge of their family in a healthy way.

You will also learn how addiction keeps you caught in denial and disbelief. Once you've read this chapter, you will have a clearer picture of how your family has shifted to accommodate unwanted behavior. You will be introduced to the habits that keep parents from moving forward and "glued" to their struggling child. This awareness will help you as you journey forward in your new Foundational Parenting approach.

Where Are My Parents?

Parents can often be physically present but unable to listen to their child without at the same time listening to an angry and distracting commentary going on in their own minds. They can zone out and become annoyed by the child's continuous demands. What the surveyed teenagers and young adults demonstrated repeatedly is that they need their parents to be emotionally present, not just physically available. They need an emotional embrace and heartfelt attention in the moment. The following poem, written by fifteen-year-old Sarah, demonstrates her yearning for her mom. Notice the emptiness in Sarah's heart. She wants her mom's attention, but her mother has emotionally checked out. Imagine how you would feel if you were Sarah. Imagine how your child would feel, too.

"Never There"

You've missed too many concerts,
You only care about my grades
Do you ever think how I feel
I'll tell you—I'm afraid
I think you think you're helping me,
But really, in fact, you don't
You told me to conform back then, you told me not to smoke
I'll tell you now, I won't
You say you'll be there
But you are off with your friends,
I'm trapped inside a nightmare
And my wits are at their ends
You don't see what I'm up against
For you compare me to the perfect child
When really no one's perfect
And compared to some, I'm mild
You tell me that I'm not depressed
Do you know me well enough to say
Because you say I never work
That all I do is play
Well, you should really do more research
Before you pass your final call
Take a good look at me
But don't get too involved this fall
So as you try to understand
Please do keep yourself distant
For I don't care much anymore
And I could change in an instant

Sarah knows what she needs from her mom. Her dad abandoned her years earlier, and her mother has been a single parent from the time Sarah was six years old. Sarah's soul is empty and lonely, and she is on the verge of ending her life. She wishes her mom would love her and pay attention to her. Instead, Sarah keeps parenting her mom and has finally given up by withdrawing emotionally.

How do I know? Sarah used to sit in my office with no energy or desire to be alive. She was also using marijuana every day and taking her friend's ADHD medication to keep herself awake. Sarah's twenty-two-year-old brother was an opiate addict and living on the streets. Sarah was failing in school, and she needed a parent's loving attention to know that she was important. Sarah ended up in the hospital for six weeks with severe depression. Her mother was part of her treatment. I saw Sarah a few times while she was hospitalized and met with her regularly for the remainder of the school year as her main support person. My message to her was that she could have a successful life even if her mom couldn't give her what she needed, and that it wasn't her fault. Her job was to find ways to connect to her school community.

Many of the teenagers I've encountered over the years share a similar story to Sarah's. All of them had been through rehab treatment, and many were also being treated for psychiatric conditions. Many were attending a recovery high school to begin experiencing life as a sober student with support from the school and classmates. They needed time to rebuild their sober self by being away from their old friends who were using, and time away from the community that had supported and enabled their addiction.

I've worked with parents who thought they had launched their young adults into the next chapter of their lives, and who were horrified to learn that their children couldn't make it due to addiction and mental health challenges. It took years for many of these parents to fully understand what was taking place. Many of them had tried some type of intervention when their children were in middle school or high school. Many of the teenagers started using during middle school and high school and hid their addiction until there were major consequences at school or in the community, including failing grades, unpaid bills, car crashes, or failing out of college.

These parents' journeys were painful and difficult, with multiple treatments, psychiatrists, therapists, family programs in treatment centers, and tremendous heartache. Many parents turned to a twelve-step fellowship for support, but they needed more help with their parenting. They needed *strategies* for turning around from the addiction to take charge of their families once again.

Parents from Different Backgrounds Share Heartfelt Emotions

The parents I have worked with came from middle-class families, wealthy families, welfare and unemployed situations, poverty, a history of chronic illness in their families, a history of depression, and/or multiple generations of addiction. They ranged in age anywhere from their thirties to their seventies. All were either in recovery themselves or part of a program because their teen, young adult, or spouse had been in treatment for addiction, mental health challenges, or both. Their hearts were aching from all the fear, sadness, and powerlessness that accompany a relationship with an addict, recovering or otherwise.

Every parent's journey was extremely painful and difficult, and usually included multiple treatments, psychiatric visits, therapy visits, and family programs at treatment centers. There was never any certainty that their loved one would remain sober and step into being a responsible person. There were no guarantees that the mental health issue would ever be resolved. Over the years, the gravity of the situation brought parents to their knees and became the focus of their whole lives. In the process, they had lost themselves to their child's addiction. If you can relate to this, please understand that it doesn't have to be this way. You *can* begin to turn things around.

Understanding Common Parenting Mistakes and Blocks

When teenagers and young adults finally get to treatment, a parent's job is just beginning. When children become sober, they will no longer fit into their families as they once did. Old patterns of behavior will not work anymore, so parents need to change as much as their children do to shift the family into a healthier dynamic in which to live and operate. Many parents share with me how easy it is to remain reactive with a child long after he or she has left treatment. "Why do I keep feeling sick to my stomach when I am around my unresponsive, angry kid? I'm sick of his attitude! Is he using again?" This parent is being pulled into her child's mood and back into old behaviors that impact every part of her being. Many of the parents in the group and parent weekends I lead share the mistakes they made when their child came home either for a visit or to live, mistakes they made because they were afraid that their child would either become angry, fail at something, or start using again. These mistakes included

- excessive nagging to get things done;
- going out of their way to get their child up for school and on time for appointments;
- yelling and putting their child down when they think differently than they do;
- being reluctant and frightened to put limits on the financial help they give to their child; and
- being fearful of enforcing house rules and boundaries.

These behaviors were based on getting through the day with an addicted child whose moods and behaviors ran daily life. However, for children to experience healthy recovery, parents need to stop letting their child's moods be in charge of them. Parents need to be in charge. The mistakes listed above illustrate parents who are giving up their parenting power to fear. Do you recognize yourself in any of these common mistakes? If so, simply be aware of them for now. With awareness, you can begin to understand why they occur and then take steps to avoid them in the future.

When addiction and addiction-related stress drive the family's dynamics, the parents' energy becomes drained and they have little if anything left for the rest of life, including for themselves. This is one of the main reasons teenagers become detached from the most significant relationship in their lives and feel blocked from their parents' true selves.

What keeps parents stuck in old mind-sets and unable to grow when faced with their child's recovery? Here are some examples:

- Thinking about the past
- Worrying about the future
- General anxiety
- Fear of negative reactions and consequences
- Hyperfocusing on a stressor or obsessing
- Inability to quiet the mind
- Not facing reality by watching television and overusing technology
- Moodiness
- Intolerance
- Impatience
- Staying overly busy
- Rushing all the time
- Yelling
- Blaming
- Hopelessness
- Powerlessness
- Secretiveness
- Shame
- Getting little to no support from others

The first step for parents is to realize that when they take on the above behaviors they tend to become powerless, worn out, emotionally bruised, and scared. Many parents have learned to simply react, worry, and give away their power to the child. They are caught in a web, and even though they try to break away from it from time to time, they tend to get pulled back into the mush. They have difficulty letting go and detaching.

When we repeat any behavior over and over, it becomes normal to us. This means that as a parent who wants things to be different, you need to challenge what feels normal to you. You need to be ready to challenge your habits and take steps into unfamiliar territory in order to realign your family dynamics. Your main job is to pay attention, catch your old habits with an "aha" smile ("Oh, I'm doing *that* again!"), and take a step back to loosen the old ways' grip on you.

Different Parents, Similar Stories

Following is a selection of case studies of parents I've met and their stories as they unfolded during our time together. Names and identifying circumstances have been changed to protect their privacy. While you may not relate to all of the details and circumstances in these narratives, try to recognize elements of your own experience in them, and think about how your own story with your child would play out if it were included here as an example for others.

Sam and Denise

Sam and Denise had four children: three teenagers and a daughter in her mid-twenties who had been using drugs, alcohol, and opiates for years. These parents were at their wits' end with rage, bitterness, and resentment toward their daughter. Addiction issues had almost destroyed their relationship. Each parent was profoundly sad, scared, anxious, furious, and disconnected from their daughter during her active addiction. Both parents were afraid to share their true emotions with the other, out of a desire to protect the other parent as well as their daughter. They could hardly stand being together anymore, and each felt very alone. They allowed their oldest daughter to become a wedge in their marriage.

Sam and Denise had many pent-up feelings, but they were unable and unwilling to share these feelings with each other. They each needed a partner but were unable to figure out how to work as a team. One parent continued to help their daughter with expenses, but the money most often went to buying heroin and street drugs. Each parent kept having to decipher their daughter's lies and deal with unpredictable behaviors, car accidents, dropping out of school, depression, and so on.

They blamed each other for their daughter's problems. Meanwhile, Sam and Denise's three other children felt betrayed and unimportant. They were totally neglected because their parents were overly focused on, and absorbed with, the addicted child.

Sam and Denise kept getting pulled into the web of addiction. They let boundaries dissolve and continued to stay hyperfocused on the addiction. Paralyzed by the thought of losing their daughter, they had been "walking on eggshells" for years, afraid of every move and unable to put a foot down and figure out a plan of action. They were unable to detach from the addiction and their daughter's unpredictable, terrifying behavior. They gave the addiction all the power in their family.

Through the 5-Step Foundational Parenting Program, Sam and Denise learned how to regain control of their family by developing new, healthier habits. When their daughter entered treatment and embarked on her road to recovery, they were able to refocus their efforts as a team on providing a more stable foundation for the entire family.

Shelly

Shelly was a single mom with an adolescent daughter whose moods were out of control. One moment she was happy, and the next she displayed manic behavior. She refused to go to school. Her drugs of choice were marijuana, opiates, meth, and anything else she could get from friends. She stole money from her mother to support her habit. Her drug use helped her cope with unstable moods, which had begun when she was in her early teens. Shelly assumed most of her daughter's acting out was due to her being a rebellious teen.

Shelly was distraught with helplessness and tried to find ways to help herself and her daughter. It took years for her daughter to get help. Most of Shelly's energy was depleted from worrying so much. She had no clue how to take charge, or which direction to take because she had brushed aside all her values. She was so afraid of her daughter's rage that she caved to all of her demands in the hope of minimizing fights and confrontations. When Shelly finally sought help for herself, she was diagnosed with depression.

When I met Shelly, she needed strategies to recover herself and to take back her parenting power. Shelly told me she was "sick and tired of being sick and tired." As her depression lifted, and with the help of the 5-Step Foundational Parenting Program, she learned healthy ways to take charge and assert her power. Her daughter eventually adhered to the family rules, and even entered treatment. Once Shelly learned to work on herself and stopped blaming her daughter for her lack of power, many healing changes took place in their relationship.

Lawrence

Lawrence came to me for help. His son, Tom, was out of treatment, age twenty-seven, and had never worked a day in his life. Tom kept making excuses for why he didn't work and kept taking and dropping out of college classes. Lawrence's denial kept this situation going on for a long time. He enabled his son with financial means as a way to compensate for the little time he was able to spend with him. Lawrence thought that Tom might be using alcohol and other drugs, but didn't know what to do. He thought if he gave Tom money, he would use less and stay enrolled in school. Tom kept manipulating his father to get more money to survive. The police eventually picked him up for speeding and possession of narcotics, and Tom went to jail.

Lawrence paid for a top-notch attorney who won the case, and all the charges were dismissed. Lawrence thought this was the wakeup call Tom needed. It wasn't.

Lawrence and his ex-wife, Tom's mother, wanted to team up to reassert their parental control but didn't know how. They felt they had lost their son and wanted him back. They thought if they gave him more money it would help, but it didn't change anything. They compromised more and more of their own values to accommodate their son's addiction. The breaking point came when Tom crashed the car and wanted his parents to pay for all the damages. His parents finally said no—and received help to get him into treatment.

Now that Tom was in treatment, Lawrence and his ex-wife needed strategies to reclaim their power and to set up clear expectations. Setting limits as a team, even though they were divorced, was critical in helping Tom stay sober. During a 5-Step Foundational Parenting weekend workshop, they agreed to work together to support Tom in his recovery, while supporting each other and being transparent in their efforts.

Jerry and Annabelle

Jerry drank all day and used stimulants to stay awake. His wife, Annabelle, kept covering for him by telling the kids that he was sick, and that that was why he never paid them any attention. Annabelle was frightened and overly focused on her husband while neglecting her children's emotional and physical needs.

George, their middle son, kept running away because he hated his home life. At age eighteen, George was smoking pot, drinking alcohol, and snorting cocaine. He felt alone in his family, as his dad was absent and his mom had withdrawn emotionally.

Annabelle kept wishing the problems would go away and couldn't see a way out of the addiction web. Then one day George was picked up by the police for driving while intoxicated. This is how he landed in treatment. George had a deep level of shame surrounding his family as well as severe attachment issues. His parents needed to heal as much as he did.

The family had never talked to anyone about their issues, but they opened up during our 5-Step Foundational Parenting family weekend. Annabelle needed strategies to take charge of her family and clarify her limits and values. She needed help to detach from the addiction and to reclaim herself. She refused to allow anyone to live in her home if they were using. As she became stronger through practice, she had an intervention with her husband and gave him an ultimatum: treatment or separation. Jerry left, and she was okay with that. However, her son recognized her strength and started respecting her. He knew that if he used again, he would either have to go back to treatment or live somewhere else. The other children also began to respect her and to feel more a part of the family. Annabelle regained her parenting power, and her children regained their mother.

All the parents in the above examples shared a number of traits and behaviors:

- Some kept trying to "buy" their children into recovery, which enabled their children to be irresponsible.
- They felt heartsick and powerless.
- They had no emotional energy left for their other children.
- They turned their backs on their own values to accommodate their child's addiction.
- They had no mental space available for anything other than their problems.
- They did not have the tools they needed to step outside the web of addiction and take charge of their families in a healthy way.

It is imperative that you understand the effects of addiction on your parenting approach and your family. Given strong evidence that addiction is passed from one generation to the next, you can make a big difference by restructuring your role to help shift your family into a healthier place. When you learn new skills as parents, you can break the intergenerational cycle of substance abuse.[2] Whether or not there is an intergenerational cycle of substance abuse present in your family, your job is to recognize how addiction has affected your family, and how the effects of addiction have shaped your parenting.

---

2 Arthur C. Evans, Jr., Roland Lamb, and William L. White, "Promoting Intergenerational Resilience and Recovery: Policy, Clinical, and Recovery Support Strategies to Alter the Intergenerational Transmission of Alcohol, Drug, and Related Problems" (Philadelphia: Department of Behavioral Health and Intellectual Disability Services), www.williamwhitepapers.com.

What About the Addicted Child's Siblings?

Many siblings of addicts share how lonely and sad they feel, having no idea what they did to push their parents away from them. They take on the brunt of the family problems. In these families the addiction of a sibling or parent is kept secret, and so it becomes the "elephant in the room." Everyone knows that something is going on, but everyone walks around the issue, they don't discuss it, and as a result everyone feels alone and left to fend for themselves.

Parents continuously and unpredictably slip away as the stressors grow, and they become caught in a loop of intensity, uncertainty, and worry. Siblings need to know they are not responsible for the problems in their families. They can't solve the problems, but they need strategies to deal with how the addiction in their families is affecting them.

Parents of these siblings can be emotionally detached and, at best, play a game of hide-and-go-seek. Sometimes they provide love and attention, but in a split second they can disappear again into their anxiety and fear for the addicted child. There is no consistency, little security, and unpredictable connection. Once in a while these children will get a dose of good parenting, only to see it vanish again when a major stressor grabs their parents from the moment. The major stressor could be thoughts associated with past encounters, thoughts of powerlessness, fear of the future, or just about anything that reminds the parent that one of his or her children is struggling with addiction. Parents unconsciously reorganize their worlds around these stressors and often hyperfocus on the problems associated with them.

The other children in the family sense the loss and feel that it is their responsibility to find ways to bring their parents back. Sometimes they try to be good, even perfect, and all grown up, ready to take over the family. These children become pseudoparents because their own parents have unconsciously abdicated their roles. They take it upon themselves to keep trying to take care of day-to-day tasks to help the family or younger siblings manage. In this way, parenting roles can become reversed, with the children parenting the parents, while the parents parent the stressor. Conversely, sometimes these children "stay little" and can't cope at all—they are filled with anxiety, depression, and fear, starving to be noticed by their parents. Many of the children I've encountered demonstrated that, often, no one was parenting them at all. Their parents were totally absorbed by the child with the addiction.

The other children in the family need as much help as the parents to learn how addiction has affected them. Take heart: when a parent engages in the 5-Step Foundational Parenting Program, everyone in the family benefits, including the "forgotten" children.

Children Aren't to Blame for a Parent's Unhappiness

Most of the teenagers I've worked with told me that they have felt responsible for their parents' moods and problems. For example, twelve-year-old Annie says, "Please remind us not to take responsibility for your feelings, thoughts, and actions. Sometimes we feel so responsible for money problems, illnesses, and your unhappiness. We need to know that we're not at fault for your feelings. Please don't blame us if you're in a bad mood. When you blame us, we feel ashamed as if there is something wrong with us deep inside and we are a bad person."

It is understandable that when you are overly focused on your child's addiction, you can lose your joy for life and, in essence, become miserable. Your misery seems to result from your child's behavior, or your child perceives it that way. Yet what really takes place in many addicted families is that parents become so enmeshed in their addicted child's life and behavior that there is no delineation between their life and emotions and their child's life and emotions. All of the unhappiness experienced seems to stem from the issue of addiction, even when other factors are present. Stressful events within the family—dealing with the addicted child among them—become the focal point for many parents. These parents can be blind to the effects the stress is having on their children; they become intolerant of the everyday needs of their children and have little patience for the people they love the most.

Rather than your operating from a place of misery, your children need you to be supportive without absorbing or personalizing their problems and taking on their feelings as your own. This means that even if your child yells at you or doesn't respond to you, you need to respond from a firm inner foundation rather than react from a feeling of depletion or unhappiness, regardless of the source.

Of course parents mean well, but they are lost—their healthy attention and attachment to their children has gone astray. How does this happen to well-meaning parents? These parents need to take steps and train themselves to detach from the addiction and learn strategies to take charge in a healthy way. Parents often feel blamed for dysfunction, yet many are just doing what is natural to them and simply need to be taught another set of skills to take charge of their families in new, productive ways. That's what the 5-Step Foundational Parenting Program will do for you. It begins with awareness and letting go of blame.

Getting Out of the Parent Trap

As we discussed and as you know firsthand, addiction can create a family atmosphere of chaos, unpredictability, inconsistency, uncertainty, changing roles, shame, fear, loss of attention, loss of emotional safety—for both parents and children—and secrecy toward the outside world. Roles change, attention changes, addiction challenges take over parents' attention. Addiction challenges are now like the parents of the family. They've taken over and control everyone. Tension, secrets, and avoiding the truth are putting a wedge in secure attachments and safe connections.

You as the parent can make a crucial shift in the family dynamic, even if your addicted child is not sober and even if there are other major stressors in the family. As painful as it may seem, parents *can* empower themselves to reclaim their true parenting roles. You can learn how to be available for the rest of your family, rather than just to your addicted child. Your other children are innocent victims who are impacted by the lack of consistent parental attention in myriad ways:

- They become overly sensitive and highly reactive to others.
- They feel on edge, filled with unexpressed and unacknowledged feelings.
- They become secretive and/or impatient.
- Their grades can suffer and they may fail to complete homework. Conversely, they might become academic overachievers and perfectionist in nature.
- Some children grow up too soon and end up parenting the parents.
- Some children stay little and are lost, lonely, and in need of lots of extra support.
- Many just feel sad and lonely and keep it hidden from the outside world, pretending everything is okay.

Parents do generally see, feel, and notice these issues, but are often too frightened to face them, preferring to avoid the situation and becoming secretive about what they truly think and feel in daily life. This avoidant, shut-down approach interferes with parents' ability to have a healthy relationship with their children. Their frustration, impatience, and sense of defeat become familiar daily feelings. However, there is no blame to be laid here. What matters is that you become aware if this is at play in your life and family, so that you can begin to make the necessary changes.

Many parents promise themselves that tomorrow will be different. For them, it's all about tomorrow—not about now. They pray and wish all the stress will go away, but nothing will change until they become present and conscious of what is currently taking place for their children. Parents tend to worry about what tomorrow will bring for their children or about what their children will become, but they forget that each child is someone *today* who needs their strength, presence, attention, and support.

Often, when teenagers or young adults leave treatment, parents haven't had a long enough opportunity to practice new approaches. They frequently continue to use old ways that have enabled their child's active addiction. When parents start to see that old ways aren't working, there is often tremendous frustration, blame, and hopelessness again. For positive change to happen, parents need information on the effects of addiction on their parenting and on their family. They need to become aware of the habits that drive their behaviors. They also need to know concretely and strategically what they can do to begin to operate as a healthy family. Stable parenting roots will lead to

- greater connection between children and their parents;
- increased opportunity for parents to support their children in rebuilding the gaps in their development, which may have been obstructed due to addiction;
- improved clarity in family rules and values;
- parenting strength and increased support for parents;
- greater attention directed toward the whole family; and
- children feeling hopeful in the family atmosphere and experiencing less blame and more support from their parents.

Becoming aware of your particular habits and unhelpful repetitive behaviors, and then letting go of or redirecting them, is an essential step in creating stable roots. Stable parenting roots ensure that your children will feel all of these integral elements of a healthy family life.

Habits and Repetitive Reactions That Keep Parents Stuck

The more conscious we are of what blocks us from being the parent we want to be, the more we can choose our actions and change our thoughts. Habits are learned and can be changed when we become aware of how they block us from what we desire. All parents were once children in their own families. They learned how to be a parent from their own parental interactions or lack thereof. This is evident whenever the words coming from our mouths sound exactly like what our own parents used to say. We feel shocked and in disbelief at what we just said. Many parents tell me how desperately they want to avoid being like their own mothers or fathers, yet their words and reactions to their children often mimic them.

Many parents have a sincere desire to parent their children differently from how they themselves were parented. Why is this so difficult? What blocks this goal are the ingrained patterns parents have picked up from their families of origin. When you understand this and catch yourself when you react in ways you promised you never would with your own family, you begin to free yourself from the past. It is possible to change your reactions and behaviors and to become the parent you dreamed of being.

Confronting the Habits That Are Keeping You Stuck
Take a look at the following list and check any that apply; feel free to add your own.
- [ ] Overly focused on worries in life
- [ ] Short-tempered/frustrated over undesired circumstances
- [ ] Impatience
- [ ] Overly committed to work, meetings, friends, or projects
- [ ] Fear of holding children accountable to family rules
- [ ] Your own mental health concerns
- [ ] You were parented poorly and don't know how to break patterns
- [ ] Knee-jerk reactions
- [ ] Hypervigilance
- [ ] Being mentally absent
- [ ] Sadness
- [ ] Fear
- [ ] Other: _____

Most often these habits have gone on for years and are so ingrained that you might struggle to recognize them. Parents' reactions can be unconscious, without awareness as to why they are repeating such self-defeating reactions to their children. They need clarity to begin to see that while they are powerless over the challenges their child's addiction creates, they are *not* powerless over themselves as parents or over their responses to their children. Through my work with parents and their children, I have learned that

- major stressors (like a child's addiction) affect parenting and as a result the whole family is affected;
- change can happen;
- families can reorganize with the proper foundations;
- parents can be effective even when they face challenges in their lives; and
- all family members can learn to live a life that is not organized around addiction.

Over the years I have received countless statements, artwork, and letters from teenagers affected by addiction expressing what it is that they need from their parents. I have synthesized them into the following five messages for parents:

1. Show up physically, emotionally, and spiritually, and be present with your children.
2. Listen, and be nonreactive with what you hear.
3. Join your children as they are and do not try to change them.
4. Be clear with family values, boundaries, and limits.
5. Play and laugh with your children and bring family spirit and rituals back to life.

These messages are the main strategies, or roots, of the 5-Step Foundational Parenting Program. These strategies will challenge the very habits that block you from being the empowered parent you want to be.

The key is to reclaim your self and to begin the journey to strengthen the foundations that will help you confront the challenges you face with your children and other stressors. When your roots—or foundations—are strong, you will be able to take charge with loving kindness, compassion, and clear boundaries, and live out your family values without absorbing your children's issues. You will be able to join your children as they are and work from a firm foundation as you practice detaching while still caring.

Parenting Insights

- Don't allow your child's moods or actions to cause reactions in you that escalate into destructive situations.
- Be clear about limits so your child will know you won't bend the rules.
- Be emotionally present, not just physically available.
- When your child enters recovery, old patterns of family behavior will cease to work. You will need to change as much as your child to shift the family into a healthier dynamic.
- Be prepared to challenge your habits and take steps into unfamiliar territory to help realign your family.
- Your other children also need help to understand how addiction has affected them.
- Be supportive without absorbing or personalizing your children's problems or taking on their feelings as your own.
- Become conscious of what blocks you from being the parent you want to be. The more aware you are, the more you will have a choice over how to act and what to think. Habits *can* be changed.

Chapter Three

Learning the Basics of the 5-Step Foundational Parenting Program

Parents whose teenagers go through the recovery process—from treatment to aftercare—witness a multitude of changes in their children. When these children leave treatment and visit or come back to live at home, they need a new family structure to feel supported in their recovery. It is important for you to adjust and restructure your parenting and family dynamics to encourage and embrace a sober household through your feelings, responses, and actions. This chapter will show you how.

The term "Foundational Parenting" represents the idea that there are specific, concrete skills parents need in order to be strong, in touch, grounded, and available to their children. When the roots are strong, the "fruits can blossom." Children are able to reach for their full potential when parents understand how to strengthen their roots by being leaders of their families with a clear plan in place.

Foundational Parenting is the antidote to being controlled by your child's addiction. The 5-Step Foundational Parenting Program will help you stabilize, anchor your parenting roots, and empower yourself as well as your entire family.

Growing Healthy Roots

Healthy roots lead to healthy growth in children and health in the family as a whole. Establishing them requires the following "nutrients" from you as the parent:

1. Learning to be present in the moment, seeing your children as they are at this moment in time—not as you wish they were. Your role as a parent is to be aware of your child's current reality and be present to him or her in that space.
2. Learning to be emotionally attuned, connected, and understanding of your child's feelings, experiences, and points of view.
3. Learning to respond, rather than react, to what you see and hear.
4. Establishing rituals and sacred family time.
5. Identifying and living the values that are important to your family and making them clear to all family members.

As we've learned, parents' actions, reactions, and fears can be "stuck" in the old addicted family patterns. This is especially true when your emotions are easily and frequently influenced by the addicted or recovering child. When you can detach from the addiction, you will have a great opportunity to strengthen your roots and build on your foundation. The following 5 Steps give you the specific strategies to transform your parenting.

STEP 1
PRACTICE BEING PRESENT WITH YOUR CHILD

"If I were a parent, I would put down my phone, turn
off the television, and stop what I was doing when
I talk to my child. I would be with them!"
—Eric, age twenty-one

Children's requests to parents: "Please pause, turn around, and be
present! Clear the space, the time, and your mind to be present with me."

Teens and young adults have shared that they feel like a burden to their parents when they want attention, help, or just to be "loved up." "Burdensome parenting" happens when parents' thoughts are in the past or the future, when they're filled with anxiety, too busy, and not mentally and emotionally present in the here and now. Children, teens, and young adults need parents to pause, turn around, and be present! That means parents need to create time for their children.

This step urges you to pause, notice, see, and be totally available in the moment when you are with your children, whether it be in person or when speaking on the phone. When you begin here, you break free of the busyness, anxieties, and stressors in your life and realign and reorganize the present moment in time. Addiction doesn't have to rob you of your usual everyday emotions or your time, energy, or brain space. You *can* stop, pause, and focus on the present moment, which gives you the freedom to connect with your family members.

Being present means:

- *Listening with full attention to your children.* This is best experienced when you are fully aware of, and present to, exactly what is happening in the moment. You are with your child in the present moment—with your thoughts, your emotions, and, when possible, your physical presence. This means consciously choosing to avoid distractions and not to mentally linger in the past or think ahead to the future. (Phones, computers, leftover projects from work, and personal anxieties are what often interfere with giving your full and undivided attention to your children.)

- *Completely accepting yourself and your child in the moment you are with them.* When parents are nonjudgmental, they experience a calmer self and less negativity. When you cultivate compassion for yourself and your children, you will discover an easier path to accepting them as they are. Compassion heals judgmental attitudes.

- *Being emotionally aware of yourself and your child when you are with them.* Take charge of your thoughts, feelings, and behaviors, knowing that you can have emotions, worries, and a busy work life and *still* choose to be present.

- *Self-regulating in the parenting relationship—staying calm even when you want to yell, cry, or storm out of the room.* To understand this, you need to notice when you are with your children and your thoughts begin to dwell on the past or you begin to worry about the future, feeling fearful of life's uncertainty. Self-regulation means you can be in charge, detach from those thought patterns, and be available to your children in the present moment. Learn to simply take note of your thoughts, emotions, and worries, and then remind yourself to return to the present moment.

Mindfulness, or being present, is paying attention on purpose, deeply and without judgment, to whatever arises in the present moment. When you practice mindfulness, you will deliberately be able to pay attention to each moment and be more available to your children. You will be less on autopilot and more conscious of negative reactions. Old ways of reacting will gradually lessen when you become mindful and catch unhelpful behaviors that produce stress, anxiety, and fear.

You will have increasing opportunities to pause and think about how you want to respond.

Most parents I work with are so busy with fear that their teen or young adult will use again that they have a difficult time being in the present moment. The following example illustrates how one parent easily tapped into her old fears when her son wasn't able to get up for school. She was on autopilot and her thoughts went back to when her son was in active addiction. She was breathing heavily, unable to distance herself, and unable to pause to gain perspective. Take a look:

Sara

Sara, mom of seventeen-year-old Sam, wanted help in the group to get clarity on expectations with her child who was just home from treatment. She wanted him to attend school every day. He had a car, and she let him drive there. One day, after four months of being sober, he was too tired to get up. She froze, wondering if he was using again. Anger welled up, followed by hopelessness, and then extreme sadness overtook her within a few moments. Sara had, again, given him all the power over her feelings. Because she was so highly reactive, she forgot that she set up a plan with her son listing expectations and consequences of him being at home after treatment. Part of this plan also identified what would take place if he didn't attend school. She needed to take a deep breath, feel her feet on the ground, and take charge. Instead, all of her emotions were triggered by his lack of responsibility, and this was the first time since he had stopped using. She overreacted and began imagining having to go through the experience all over again.

If this has happened to you, fear not. The following steps show what you can do to reverse direction and arrive back in the present moment.

Four Steps to Being in the Present Moment

1. Pause, notice, see the situation in front of you as it is, and take a deep breath.

2. Ground yourself by placing your attention on your feet firmly rooted to the floor beneath you.

3. As you notice an old habit that produces anxiety or stress inside you or just thoughts that won't stop, catch yourself by taking a deep breath. Again, feel your feet on the ground to come back to the present moment.

4. Become aware when your mind gets busy, and gently come back to the now as many times as you need to. Respond to whatever is happening from this place of present awareness.

Distractions to Being Present

We have become a generation of busybodies—on the phone, on screens, texting, overly involved with work, and missing our kids' school events. Becoming aware of generational busyness can help parents stop and take back their families. Often teens and young adults share with me that they feel unimportant and as though they don't count because their parents are always too busy to really pay attention to them—to really hear what they have to say. Over time, our children begin to pull back and mourn the loss of their parents. Parents generally don't mean to back away from their children, but they are very much caught up in their own worlds. They often forget that their children want *them*, whether it's in person, on the phone, at mealtimes, or when they are visiting.

Action Step:

Where are you with regard to being present with your children? Ask yourself the following questions and record your answers in a journal or notebook.

What does being present with your children mean to you?

How present are you with your children now?

How does it compare to when they were in active addiction?

How did addiction and other major stressors prevent you from being present for your family?

What pulls you away from parenting with presence in the moment (for example, anger, resentments, fear, anxiety)?

How does your being physically present but not emotionally present affect your children?

How can you use this step to strengthen your parenting?

What might stand in the way of you being present for your children moving forward?

How will you notice when you are not present for your children? What are the clues?

What can you do to be more present each day?

Use these questions to take a look at where you were with regard to being present when your child was in active addiction. When you see where you have been, you can make the conscious decision to show up differently each day for your child in recovery and for other members of your family. Noticing, understanding, and being aware of what interrupts your presence can help you catch those interferences in order to practice being available for your family from here on.

STEP 2
BECOME EMOTIONALLY ATTUNED TO YOUR CHILDREN

"I would never be overbearing when my kids are upset.
I would just listen instead of trying to fix them. We
remember when you listen and accept what we have to say."
—Jerry, age twenty-five

Children's request to parents: "Please listen to me and don't jump in and try to change what I'm saying. Listen and validate my feelings and don't try to change them; otherwise, I will shut down. Stay emotionally attuned; understand my point of view. When I feel unheard, I shut down and become resentful, embarrassed, detached, and hopeless. But when you listen to me and I feel heard, my heart opens up and I feel relief."

This step teaches parents to listen to their children's point of view. This does not mean you have to *agree*. Simply *listen and understand where they are coming from with their opinions, thoughts, and feelings.* Your real job is to be present to your children and acknowledge what you see and what you hear as their truth. Your role is to see them as they are, *not as you wish they would be.* Put aside your feelings and thoughts and join your children as they are in the moment to really witness them.

If you use any of the following statements with your children, become aware that you are shaming them and not accepting their reality. Phrases like these can feel like a big putdown to your kids and can negatively affect them in many ways. Shame can destroy relationships because it severs the bridge to healthy attachment.

How can you think that way?
What's wrong with you?
Are you crazy?
You shouldn't feel that way.

When you make these statements, or versions of them, you aren't hearing your child's perspective on a situation. This isn't about how you, the parent, think and feel; it's about how your child thinks and feels. Your role is to learn to listen, understand, and not react to what you hear. Your children need to have their own thoughts, feelings, and reactions. The greatest gift you give them is to understand their point of view and acknowledge what you hear.

One parent I worked with provides an excellent example. Her son was twenty-three. He had dropped out of college due to failing grades. His trust fund was gone as a result of his addiction. He was addicted to opiates and had been through multiple treatments. During a family program, this mother brought up to other parents how upset she was with his "crazy ideas." She had begun yelling at him and was feeling quite guilty and remorseful. Now her son wanted her to buy him a car so he could drive to the beach every day and play guitar and collect money that way.

I reminded her that he probably stopped growing developmentally when he began using heavily in tenth grade. Now that he was sober, he was dreaming, and her role was simply to listen, understand, and not feel responsible for making things happen for him. She was always afraid of his rage. Being present taught her to listen to her son and not overreact to what she heard. Of course she had to *learn* how to keep her immediate reactions to herself and how to only be present. That was *her* job. Her son's job was to figure out how to go forward in life, earn money, and be responsible.

Often, teenagers and young adults developmentally "redo" or catch up to some of their earlier stages of development that were interrupted when they began using. Your job as the parent is to notice and support their journey, whatever stage that may be. What doesn't change is the need for you to be clear about what your values are, how your family operates, and what role you will play in your child's life financially.

Children, regardless of their age, are unique individuals with their own hearts, souls, thoughts, and feelings. They feel respected and validated when we listen to them wholeheartedly. We don't have to agree; we first need to understand.

Being emotionally attuned to our children is critical if we want healing to take place in our families. This step teaches parents to focus on their children by listening with their whole being and understanding their children's point of view. Understanding doesn't mean agreeing or disagreeing. Understanding means you simply acknowledge, accept, and understand. All children want to be understood and listened to without their parents butting in with reactions, facial expressions, stiff body language, and so on. When parents are attuned to their children, the children feel heard and connected to their parents. This is critical for children to feel vibrant, alive, understood, and at peace. It only happens if the parent is *present*.

Being present as discussed in Step 1 helps parents listen to their children without judging the thoughts, opinions, and emotions they might share. When parents show up and really listen sincerely to their children, an important "heartfelt connection" takes place.

Children want you to acknowledge what they feel and give it a name—not try to change it. This starts as early as infancy. The baby cries; you notice and acknowledge the crying and figure out a way to help. When something else takes precedence and interferes with the parent's presence, the message changes to "Stop crying! I can't handle this."

Think about this for a moment. Remember a time you felt upset about something and someone told you not to feel bad about it. How did that make you feel? They were trying to control how you felt and told you what you were feeling was wrong. Though well-intentioned, this approach rarely helps the receiver feel better. We need to join our children as they are, understand how they feel, and acknowledge it. Too often parents tell their children not to worry so much and to get over their upset feelings. We parents give our viewpoints and thereby inadvertently invalidate what our children are telling us about their reaction to something. Our job is to understand our children and not change what we hear.

Too often we feel pressed for time and anxious for everyone to just "be happy," which leads us to become impatient, intolerant, and selfish. Frequently we put too much pressure on ourselves, feeling the weight of the responsibility to "fix" what is bothering our children. The trick is to relinquish that responsibility, and to free yourself of that burden. Instead, realize that your children simply need you to hear, acknowledge, and accept what they are expressing. There is nothing for you to do other than bear witness to their experiences, without judgment. Doing this creates a greater bond and a closeness of the heart, and magically reduces conflict.

To recap: listen, acknowledge, and understand your child's point of view. It is critical to rebuilding a healthy environment for your family. Your body posture and facial expressions can either envelop your child with understanding and attunement or shame him or her into feeling they are "wrong, deep inside." No parent consciously desires to harm their children, which is why this step of understanding and listening is key to reestablishing a trusting relationship that allows for the flourishing of true connection between you and your child.

Action Step:

How can you strengthen your emotional attunement with your child? Reflect on where you currently are in relation to this step by asking yourself the following questions and responding in a notebook or journal.

What does "emotionally attuned" mean to you?

Why is this step important in rebuilding your relationship with your child?

How attuned were you with your child during the active addiction?

What are you doing to rebuild your relationship with your child?

If you are having a difficult time listening to and understanding your child's point of view, what stands in your way?

How can parents really listen to and understand their children? How would listening and understanding change your family dynamics?

Imagine someone is listening to you with unconditional positive attention, validating your perspective, and understanding your thoughts and feelings. What is it like to be "felt" like this by another person? How might living in an addicted family have sabotaged this experience?

How will you use this step to strengthen your parenting?

When you were in the middle of dealing with the active addiction, what happened to this strategy?

How can you prevent obstacles from interfering with this strategy moving forward?

This is a vital step in your journey toward healing your relationship with your children. The above questions are designed to give you pause and inspire reflection to really look at your patterns of relating to your children—first when they were in active addiction, and now that they are in recovery. Your task is to practice listening and understanding your children without judgment. Understand that they are entitled to their own ways of thinking, feeling, and acting. When parents begin to model this step by refraining from criticizing or belittling their children, a new bond of trust can emerge. When you take the time to listen wholeheartedly and understand without judgment, a mutual respect and appreciation can begin to redevelop in your parent-child relationship.

STEP 3
RESPOND TO YOUR CHILDREN WITHOUT JUDGMENT

*"Our ultimate freedom is the right and power to decide
how anybody or anything outside ourselves will affect us."*
—Stephen Covey

**Children's request to parents: "Please don't put me down. If you
disagree with something I do or something I share with you, don't
shame me. I need you to stop overreacting to me. I don't want the
power to make you upset; I want you to be okay even if I struggle.
Don't give me the power to push your buttons. Please don't make it my
job to take care of you emotionally. I want you to be able to show up,
notice me, and take care of me."**

Children have their own point of view—we don't have to agree—
yet they need us to listen and not react, no matter how wrong or even
dangerous we feel their thinking is. When we try to change how they
see something or how they feel, our buttons get pushed, and we are no
longer seeing their reality. When we overreact to what we see and hear,
we end up shaming our children and making them feel like bad people.
Judging hurts all relationships.

In families affected by addiction, impatience and intolerance
can prevent parents from really getting to know their children. Often,
parents can't stop, pause, see, hear, and be present because they are
so absorbed by the family's struggles and challenges. Most parents
have lost the patience to really be available. In addition, parents tend
to be convinced that they are right and their children are wrong. This
is unhelpful black-and-white thinking. Instead, the key is to see your
children, hear them, and join them as they are—not as you wish they
would be. Remember, your values and rules of how you manage your
children are essential in transforming your family. Listening to your

children's point of view lets them know that you understand how they think and feel. It's not about changing that; it's about listening, acknowledging, and understanding.

Witness and observe your children without judgment. Take the time to be available to respond to their needs by communicating, listening, and paying attention. If your children don't respond to you the way you wish they would, don't react in frustration. Take a deep breath, and remember that your role is to stay grounded in your own strength. Do not react and create conflict from a place of fear or anger. Calm yourself, center yourself, take care of yourself. You are in control, and you have the right to make sure your family's values and boundaries are respected—on your terms. Let your children know you are ready to talk when they are, and then back away.

Remember, the only thing you can change is yourself and how you respond. As you begin to be more present, be more attuned, and practice not reacting so quickly to something you don't like, you will notice your children begin to trust you more. They, too, will realize that your actions, your words, and your intentions match.

Parents need to learn how to show up, take charge, listen, and be nonjudgmental with their children's differing points of view. Parents need to practice noticing how they respond to their children and recognize that they *can* choose not to be reactive. The ability to respond in flexible ways is one of the most important skills of being a parent. It means having the capacity to sort through a wide variety of reactions— including impulses, ideas, and feelings—that come up in a conscious, self-aware, and *nonautomatic* manner, as opposed to giving in to routine reactions. Routine reactions are the knee-jerk, unhelpful responses to children's thoughts, behaviors, and emotions that occur when we are not present in the moment.

Interestingly, knee-jerk reactions happen more frequently when parents are hungry, angry, lonely, and/or tired. The acronym HALT refers to these four states while at the same time reminding you of what to do if you are experiencing one or more of them: if you notice you are hungry, angry, lonely, or tired, HALT!—meaning pause, step back, don't react, and take time to respond.

HALT has been used by twelve-step fellowships for a long time, and is now a well-recognized tool of recovery. Whenever you are feeling low or in distress, turn to the first step of Foundational Parenting: pause and bring yourself into the present moment. If you are having difficulty listening to your child and feel highly reactive, tap into the second step to listen more and self-regulate your emotions.

You have a choice. You don't have to fall back on old, automatic responses. Take a moment and figure out how to be available and hear what your child is saying by halting your initial reaction. In other words, pause, and then regroup your thoughts and decide on your actions. You may decide that you need time to think about what your child just said. Teenagers tend to want parents to respond immediately, but remember that *you* are in charge. You can pull back for as long as you need to in order to get clarity on the situation and come up with a response that is in harmony with your grounded self.

In highly stressed families, there can be a lot of uncertainty, intolerance of differences, and lack of patience. All the attention typically goes toward the stressor and away from the children, which is when judgment of the situation and the children can rear its ugly head. Parents can work to create a different strategy to support their children by turning attention away from the stressor. Acknowledge the cause of trouble, but don't let it take control of everything that happens. The initial step here is to become self-aware, and to redirect your attention to your children, without judgment, while also not taking on or absorbing their thoughts and feelings.

How do you go about doing this? A reframing of Step One of the twelve-step fellowships can help you separate yourself from your children's thoughts, feelings, and problems: "I am powerless over others' thoughts, feelings, actions, and problems. I am in charge of my thoughts, feelings, actions, and problems. I can see, hear, and witness my kids, but I do not have to absorb their difficulties."

Five Methods to Practice Nonjudgment

1. Recognize and reflect on the importance of you and your child having your own separate and distinct thoughts, feelings, actions, and challenges in your daily lives.

2. Recognize and reflect on the fact that you can think and feel differently from how your child does about any given situation.

3. Be clear about your values, expectations, and boundaries as a family (Step 5 will delve more deeply into this). You can listen wholeheartedly to your children's arguments and differing viewpoints about a rule in the family, and you can understand why they think the way they do, all the while staying true to your values and not budging on rules. This can be done calmly and without hostility.

4. If you notice you are getting defensive and angry, and are telling yourself negative things about your children, pause and take a break. It simply means you need to feel your feet on the ground, focus on your breathing, and come back to the present moment.

5. If you notice you are becoming negative and blaming your children for your problems—catch yourself, apologize immediately, and take a break. Tell them you are really trying to listen more and understand their point of view. If your child storms off out of anger or frustration, tell him or her you would like to continue the conversation and hear their point of view when they are ready.

Action Step:

In what ways can you strengthen your ability to respond rather than react to your child? To see where you are with this step, ask yourself the following questions and respond in a notebook or journal.

What does responding really mean? How can it be applied to reorganizing your family?

What stands in the way of you taking your time to listen without your buttons getting pushed?

Think of an example when you were really upset with one or more of your children. Remember and reflect on how you handled it.

Can you remember any times when you did not immediately react to something that made you upset? If so, list some examples.

How can you listen to another point of view that you don't agree with without getting upset?

How do the challenges you now face affect your ability to respond to your children's needs?

How did you deal with the emotions you carried with you when your child was using? Reflect on whether you were able to acknowledge those feelings and own them, or you blamed and "let your feelings out" on others.

When you listen more, and pause before responding thoughtfully, what changes do you notice in your children?

How is this step helpful to you as your child begins his or her recovery journey?

Reflect on how the following statement will help you in responding rather than reacting: *I am powerless over other people's emotions and problems. I am in charge of my emotions, reactions, and my actions.*

This step teaches you to embrace your children by understanding their point of view no matter what it is they share with you. Often teenagers want to get a rise out of their parents, and applying this step will take the wind right out of their sails. They will no longer have the power to cause you to react to their words and behaviors. This step teaches you to pause and redirect your energy by first reflecting and then responding to what you see and hear, instead of being in a combative mood and shutting your children out with old, negative thinking. Being responsive, rather than reactive, puts respect back into your relationship with your whole family, including your child in recovery.

STEP 4
CREATE SACRED FAMILY TIME

"I missed our celebrations in the past few
years since I was out of it and addicted.
Please make this important again in our family."
—Roger, age eighteen

Children's request to parents: "Please show up and relate to me with a light spirit, gentleness, and compassion. Create sacred space and time with me so we can play and laugh. Don't give up, even if I don't immediately join in. I want you to rekindle that spirit that makes families come alive and trust that you will be consistent and follow through with what you say. It's never too late to have a happy childhood!"

Sacred family time is critical for reestablishing trust. It's your responsibility to begin to put lightheartedness back into your family, as intensity has likely ruled much of the time during your child's active addiction and the many stressors it brought. Events were probably canceled due to fear, sadness, and anger. As you take back your family and begin to parent with empowerment, you have the wonderful opportunity to create shared sacred experiences again, such as holidays, birthday celebrations, and special family time. Such occasions and traditional rituals can help your family heal. Keep in mind that one person's mood doesn't have to control what's important to you. You can still celebrate, even if not everyone is present.

Take this as a special opportunity to get clarity on and reassert what is important to you as a parent. Be fully present and intentional, letting everyone know about holidays, birthdays, and special events that matter to you. Do not cancel an event that is important to you due to someone else's moods, use of chemicals, or poor behavior. Your job is to show up for what matters most to your family, to follow through with celebrations, and to not let other things interfere.

Family rituals create a sense of belonging. They let everyone in the family know what's important, and give every family member a sense of identity. Rituals and ceremonies can also be special events that only your family puts on. They help communicate and reassert that "this is who we are," giving all family members a grounding, comforting, and healing sense of belonging.

Five Ways to Create or Reestablish Family Rituals

1. Ask your teenagers and young adults about their favorite holiday to celebrate as a family. If you don't have children who live at home, call them to gather this information. You could even have a conference call on the phone or video chat with everyone.

2. Ask for each family member's commitment to weekly check-in times as a family. This can become a "standing appointment" that everyone agrees to. If your children do not live at home, find a mutually agreeable time to connect each week to reestablish your relationship and sacred time to communicate. Video chatting is always an option if there is significant geographic distance between you.

3. Discuss with your family special times during the year that are sacred to you, including birthdays, holidays, vacations,

and so on, where everyone has an opportunity to be together. Ask what each person considers special times for your family. Poll your family members to see what they like to do when everyone is together, such as creating time for a special meal, playing games, going to movies, and/or inviting other family members and friends over. Gather everyone's input. One parent needs to take charge to write up what comes out of the discussion and share it with everyone, by email, for example.

4. Rituals can revolve around distinctive meals that are eaten together as a family during special times. If you don't have established favorite family dishes, ask everyone what their favorite foods are and find a way to make those foods available when you share meals together.

5. As your family is recovering from addiction, there is a lot of forgiveness that will need to take place. Be sure to acknowledge past difficulties and express the importance of having family time again. To be successful, you will need to determine what will work for your family, and your family specifically, and don't give up. Celebrate baby steps, such as a first gathering, no matter how brief.

Action Step:

In what ways can you strengthen your family's participation in and enjoyment of rituals? To see where you are with this step, ask yourself the following questions and respond in your journal or notebook.

> Reflect on sacred family time in the past when you used to play and laugh together. How did life stressors interrupt or bring these times to an end?

> Do you now plan time in your day to just be together as a family without interruptions? If so, what does that look like?

What types of family rituals do the members of your family participate in? If none at this time, then what rituals would you like to create for your family?

What do you do together with your family that's fun?

What makes you laugh with your children?

Can you find humor throughout the day, or are you too busy with work or life challenges?

How can rituals and sacred family time help you connect with your children?

What are little things you can do each day to feel more connected to your children?

How do you create sacred time and space for your children?

How can you "have sunshine" amid challenging times? How might you still be able to enjoy this time even if there are major stressors?

This step helps you put together a new plan to create and/or recreate sacred family time during which to connect with each other and practice being together in your new, sober environment. During your child's active addiction, intensity and drama may have often taken over family celebrations, interrupting birthdays, holidays, and other special occasions. The above questions are designed to help you assess where you were in the past, where you are now, and where you want to go from here with regard to sacred family rituals and special family bonding times. Carving out sacred family time is the most important thing you can do to strengthen your relationship with your children and support them in their recovery.

STEP 5
CLARIFY VALUES, RULES, AND BOUNDARIES

"Parents who are afraid to put their foot
down usually have children
who step on their toes."
—Chinese proverb

Children's request to parents: "Please use kindness and compassion with me. Stick to clear boundaries. I need to know how our family operates and that I can be safe emotionally, spiritually, and physically. I need to know what's important in our family and that you won't budge with certain rules, even if I don't like them. You don't have to change a rule because I disagree. How you disagree with me and treat my spirit is the key to helping our family feel whole and happy again."

All parents have the right and the privilege of defining what is important to them and then living by the values they wish for their families. Regardless of their age, teenagers and young adults need to be clear on these family values, rules, and boundaries, and the consequences that will occur if they break a rule or cross a line. When parents are available emotionally and physically, they can reinforce the limits and values in their families. Children need parents to be in charge in a loving, caring way while reinforcing rules and setting clear boundaries. Keep in mind that there are both spoken and unspoken rules and values in every family.

Reflect on the following questions to evaluate where you currently stand with your family's values and boundaries:

- What is each person's role in your family?
- How can you live life according to your values, without compromising them?

- How can you set up boundaries and hold your kids accountable?
- What happens when you ignore your values because you "just want peace"?
- What roles do your children play in defining your family rules and values?
- What do you do when your children cross the line? Are they clear about what that line is?
- What are the principles that guide your children day to day?

Addiction in the family often keeps us from living life according to our own values. As parents begin to rebuild their foundation, it is imperative that they define what those values are, and what values they expect every member of the family to uphold. Keeping this in mind on a daily basis and refusing to tolerate it when boundaries are crossed or rules are broken builds consistency. Over time, staying firm on values, boundaries, and rules reestablishes trust in families.

Teenagers depend on their parents for guidance and unconditional love. It requires a lot of present-centered interactions, nonjudgmental attention, and compassion. One of the keys to success for teenagers and young adults in recovery is to provide them with a clear understanding and awareness of the value system that is in operation in your family.

Clarity of values where everyone "walks the walk" is critical for the healthy reorganization of families in recovery. Teenagers need their parents to embrace and live by their values and boundaries as key guidelines in their recovery. To reestablish a healthy family, your children need you to be present, to support them and hear them, to keep the boundaries clear, and to keep them safe. The best way to teach values is through your own example.

Parents often find they have leftover reactions from their own childhoods that can interfere with their dreams becoming reality. Even if your childhood was difficult, you are free to change the rules today. You *can* turn around and create what you desire in your family. As a parent, you have the privilege of deciding what is important to you and how you want your family to operate as you go forward, beginning today.

Identify Your Values

To see where you are with this step, think of the values you have in each of the following areas of life, and write them down in a journal or notebook. A value can be anything that is important to you, such as a principle (for example, "every time X happens, I expect Y to happen"), a code of morals (for example, "I will never tolerate X" or "I demand Y no matter what"), or certain standards (for example, "In my friendships I expect . . .").

1. Using drugs/alcohol
2. Schoolwork/higher education
3. Family time
4. Communication
5. Helping
6. Independence
7. Money
8. Chores
9. Mealtimes
10. Holidays
11. Kindness
12. Spirituality
13. Emotions
14. Friendships

Think back to how stressors such as illness, divorce, mental health challenges, or active addiction in your family have blocked you from living life according to your own true values. Think of real-life situations that have interfered with your ability to parent with power from a place of personal integrity (being in alignment with what matters to you most). Values that are clear and that you are consciously aware of have a powerful impact on decisions you make and the actions you take as a parent. There is no shortcut or substitute for defining and expressing your values so that you can demonstrate, practice, and live life according to what is most important to you. To get your family back on track and into alignment with your values, you need to identify what is important to you and take that as your new base of operation.

Action Step:

To see where you currently are as a family, and to identify where you want to be, ask yourself the following questions and respond in your journal or notebook.

What happened to your family rules and values when your child was in active addiction?

What values are important to you in your family now?

What are nonnegotiable limits for your children?

Why is it important for you to have clear personal boundaries with your children? What do these boundaries look like?

How do clear personal boundaries protect your children emotionally, physically, and sexually?

Are you consistent with your rules/limits so your children know what you mean and that you mean what you say?

What happens when you can't live up to what is important to you?

How have your values/boundaries and family structure changed since recovery?

> What are the ways in which your children violate, or could violate, your family rules and values?
>
> When your children step over the line, how do you handle it?
>
> How can you embrace your children's spirit while providing consistent consequences for breaking of rules?

The children I have worked with have made it clear that they want their parents to be in charge, and I believe this is true for all children. Parents need to create a safe and healthy climate in the family by being transparent with the values that are important to them and the expectations or rules that everyone is to adhere to. To guide and support your family, state up front and explicitly what you expect. In my work I often see children being given too much power in negotiating family rules when what they really want and need is clarity and for their parents to stick to what they say. So, even if your teen or young adult argues against a rule or dislikes what you set up, know that he or she really doesn't want you to betray your own values. Your children want you to be in charge even if they make a fuss. When you change a rule or skirt your values in response to their complaint or behavior, it gives them too much power, which can paradoxically make them feel unsafe and out of control.

You, as the parent, have the right and the privilege to determine what values, rules, and principles will guide your actions and expectations in your family unit. When these are crystal-clear and consistently enforced, everyone can grow and live with a greater sense of safety, trust, and joy.

Putting the 5 Steps of Foundational Parenting Together

The 5 Steps help you shift your parenting and take charge of your family again. As you practice each step, notice how your children respond. In Chapter 2, we looked at habits that keep parents stuck in their old patterns. Feel free to revisit that chapter any time to remind yourself of the importance of interrupting outdated, unhealthy behaviors as soon as they occur. Become aware of and let go of any habits that block you from being present, emotionally attuned, and able to respond to your children from a strong foundation. When you notice them, remember to pause, smile, and identify the step that will help you the most in that situation. Remember to listen, be present, respond, and take all the time you need to get grounded, protect your heart, and not react automatically to your children's thoughts, feelings, or behavior.

Your job is to notice your children's feelings, actions, and challenges—without judgment. Remember that these belong to your children. You have your own feelings, actions, and challenges. Second, define and remember the values that guide you and your family and work diligently to keep your words, actions, and behaviors aligned with your value system so your children know when they step over the line.

In Chapter 4, we will look at concrete strategies to practice these steps to reclaim your family from addiction and reclaim your parenting power.

Parenting Insights

- The 5 Steps of Foundational Parenting will help you stabilize, grow your parenting roots, and empower yourself as well as your family, despite the challenges and stressors you face.
- When you detach from the addiction of a family member, you have a unique opportunity to strengthen your roots and build your parenting foundation.
- Your teen or young adult needs you to pause, turn around, and be present. You need to create time for your children.
- When you cultivate compassion for yourself and your children, you discover an easier path to accepting them as they are. Compassion dissolves judgments.

- Your job is to see your children as they are and acknowledge what you see and what you hear as their truth. Your role is to see them as they are, *not* as you wish they would be.
- All children are individuals. They feel respected and validated when we listen wholeheartedly. We don't have to agree; we need first to understand.
- Body postures and facial expressions can either embrace children with empathy or shame them into thinking they are "wrong deep inside."
- Take the time to listen wholeheartedly, so that trust can redevelop in your parent-child relationship.
- The only thing you can change is yourself and how you respond. As you become more present and attuned, you will see your children trusting you more and realizing that your actions, your words, and your intentions match.
- As you take back your family and begin to parent with strength, embrace the opportunity to reestablish or newly create sacred family experiences, such as holidays, birthdays, and other special occasions.
- It is imperative that you define what values are important to you, and be clear about the rules and boundaries you expect family members to live by.
- Be firm and unwavering in upholding your values, rules, and boundaries. It is essential to reestablishing trust in your family.

Chapter Four

Putting the 5-Step Process to Work for You

Y ou are now ready to step forward in your parenting journey. In this chapter you will learn how to use the 5 Steps to disentangle yourself and your family from the web of addiction and reintroduce yourself as a parent in charge. You will also discover an adapted version of the "Stages of Change Model" by Prochaska and DiClemente. Its Seven Stages will help you understand where you are as a parent on your journey to fostering sustainable recovery in your family system.

Always remember that you are powerful. Parents make a big difference in their children's lives. While years of pain and broken hearts caused by addiction can rule family life, family decisions, and family rituals it doesn't have to stay this way. Know that you can learn to resist being absorbed by your child's addiction, and that it is possible to consciously and intentionally step back into healthy parenting and a healthy life.

The most important thing I learned from working with hundreds of teens and young adults is that the vast majority of them truly desire a healthy, supportive relationship with their parents. Parents are sometimes shocked to hear this because they don't see their real child behind the addiction. Even when the child enters recovery, it can take a while for these parents and their children to experience the transformation that can take place in their lives. The family system has typically been so undermined by addiction issues that parents don't have the skills and strategies needed to shift the family toward health and well-being. Making such a shift begins with parents believing that they can make a difference by being present and nonjudgmental, and by listening to their children's viewpoints without reacting.

Where to Begin

To step forward and take new actions, you need to know where to begin. So often I see parents promise themselves they will do things differently and then fail to keep that promise. Progressing on a recovery path requires conscious intention and deliberate action each and every day. It also requires support. Too many times throughout my years of working with parents of addicts I've watched parents try and fail to maintain new strategies without the necessary help and guidance.

Panic, fear, hopelessness, and codependency are the roadblocks that stop parents on the path toward change. There is a sincere desire to do whatever it takes to help their children stay and thrive in recovery, but it so often comes at the expense of the parents' true values and boundaries, in which case all efforts are in vain. Parents give themselves up and become lost in the process. They are often stuck in their own emotions and paralyzed before they even start the process. Parents need concrete information and specific guidance to empower themselves to take the first steps in a new direction. When parents know where to begin and are clear about their goals, they can make intentional, sustainable improvements to their relationships with their children.

The following seven stages provide a roadmap for your journey in relationship to your addicted child. Use it to help you identify where you're currently at, by seeing what stages you've already experienced, and which still lie ahead for you. Once you see what stage you're in, you will know where to begin and what next steps to focus on in moving your family further along the road to recovery.

THE SEVEN STAGES

Stage One: Blaming the Teen or Young Adult for Family Problems

In this stage, parents are blind to the effects of addiction on their families. All they can do is blame their child or children for all the family problems. There is shame and embarrassment about the addicted children, and parents try to deny any part they play in the family dysfunctions. Common attitudes at this stage are

- *If only my child weren't addicted, we would be okay.*
- *It's my husband's fault,* or *It's my wife's fault.*
- *It's our divorce.*
- *If my partner didn't keep bailing him out and giving him money, we would be okay.*
- *I'm fine the way I am. It's my kid who wrecks our family.*

The blame is placed on everyone else and on each other, instead of looking at oneself and looking at what one could do to improve one's parenting and take charge differently.

Parents at this stage don't recognize how addiction is affecting their parenting and their child. When teenagers or young adults face challenges in their own lives, their troubles and behaviors are written off as typical for their age and merely indicative of a child trying to find his or her way in the world. However, as concerns for the child's health and safety begin to grow, parents at last begin to enter the second stage.

Stage Two: Thinking About the Problems but Feeling Unable to Take Action to Make Changes at Home

Parents at this stage are beginning to see more of reality, but they keep most of the information in their heads. They aren't ready to take action, and are still in denial about the fact that their child needs help. Parents increasingly think about the challenges they face in their family, but they're unable to take action. Anxieties are not expressed outwardly, but kept hidden inside bodies that ache with fear and worry. Many parents at this stage focus on what they observe with their children as they witness them disappearing, emotionally and physically, from their family. Tensions mount and begin to take a toll on everyone. Parents are not yet seeking help and are at a loss as to what they can do.

I've heard many parents say that they knew something was going on for a long time with their children and that they suspected drug abuse of some kind, but felt unable to do anything. As one parent put it, "I was in so much denial about Jon's drug usage. When money was missing from my wallet for the tenth time, I finally had a wake-up call. I needed to stop pretending that everything would be okay in time." When the signs become too hard to ignore and parents reach the point of being "sick and tired of being sick and tired," they are ready to move on to the next stage.

Stage Three: Seeking Help and Information Through Books, Online Searches, Interventions, Therapy, and Friends

Parents at this stage are actively looking for help. Most teenagers and young adults don't go into treatment of their own volition, and parents at this point are willing to do almost anything to step forward and interrupt the addiction. They are now able to choose to receive help because they see their family disintegrating. Feeling isolated and ashamed of what is taking place at home is replaced with a growing understanding of addiction as a universal experience. Parents now see that they aren't alone and that many other families have similar issues. Still, parents feel powerless and in need of professional help. Once they gather enough empowering information and professional guidance, they become open to making decisions that recognize addiction as a family disease. Eventually parents take action to address the addiction and the role their family plays in it. Many families now prepare for an intervention to get their children into treatment.

Stage Four: Taking Steps to Begin Self-Work and Address the Challenges with the Child

At this stage, parents learn new strategies and skills to help them reclaim their parenting from the web of addiction. Typically the addicted child has entered some form of treatment and several, if not all, family members are participating in a family recovery program. It is the parents' exposure to education and therapy that opens the possibility of family recovery. For parents who aren't part of their child's treatment program, many other types of help and support are available, including twelve-step fellowships, individual and couples' therapy, workshops, classes, and treatment programs designed specifically for codependency. When parents experience the initial relief from the fear, shame, and anxiety that they've carried for years, they can begin the work of detaching and of taking charge differently in their families. Now parents are ready to enter Stage Five.

Stage Five: Sustaining New Strategies to Maintain a Recovering Family

It is at this stage that parents benefit most from the 5-Step Foundational Parenting Program. The 5 Steps guide parents in learning to detach from the addiction and their child's addicted behaviors. They also teach parents how to listen to their children without absorbing their emotions, challenges, and problems. To become a healthier, recovering family, parents learn to clarify their values and define how they will operate as a family in recovery. It's when families leave their child's treatment program that the real work begins. Family weeks and weekend programs will begin to touch on some of the pain and deceit caused by addiction. Before a teen or young adult leaves treatment, he or she typically puts together a relapse plan with the team of counselors and clinicians, as well as his or her parents. Treatment programs also equip the newly sober person with plans and strategies to put his or her life back together again. When a child's treatment program does not include parents, it is advisable for them to seek other guidance in creating new expectations as well as a relapse plan. Without such a plan, parents will be left hanging without any help to decide what to do if their child relapses. (Chapter Six will delve further into relapse planning and prevention.) At this stage, having practiced new action steps, new behaviors, and new ways of taking charge, parents have an opportunity to reclaim themselves.

Stage Six: Reclaiming One's Self

At this stage, parents are no longer trapped by their child's addictive behaviors or their own current or past emotions. Parents have regained their freedom by consciously working on their own program with specific strategies that empower them as a parent in their family. When parents recognize and accept that they are powerless over their child's addiction, emotions, and challenges, they begin to feel a heavy weight lifting from their shoulders. They are no longer bound by their teen or young adult's moods, demands, or requests. They now recognize that they can be in charge in a healthier way and are able to take back their parenting power.

At this stage, you begin to "regain yourself" and empower your parenting by using well-practiced tools whenever you feel stuck, such as pausing, stopping, untangling, and separating from the addiction web, your child's reactions, and the stresses surrounding you. You *can* be grounded and in charge again. Your freedom to regain yourself becomes easier and easier the more you separate and disengage from your adolescent or young adult. You no longer have to absorb his or her feelings, problems, or challenges. However, it is easy for parents to slip back into old, familiar behaviors, especially when new and challenging situations arise with their child. Stage Seven lays out how parents can consciously notice when they are getting off track and provides the necessary tools to step forward again in the right direction.

Stage Seven: Relapsed Parenting

In this stage, parents go back to reacting to their children like they did when their children were in the grip of active addiction. Instead of taking charge and living within the values and boundaries they have defined, parents have steered off their path due to fear and hopelessness. They have once again become trapped in obsessive thinking about their child's every move. As fear, anger, and panic take over their actions, parents are again "stuck in the muck."

One client, Sharon, a parent of a young adult, perfectly illustrated this stage when she shared the following in a group: "My son went through treatment many times and lived in a sober-living home, so I thought I'd learned to listen, and not react so quickly. Many times, though, I would hear a crazy idea of his and I flip out with what he was telling me. My eyes would open wider, my body would become stiff, and I was immediately drawn back into his world. I'm learning how to protect myself and not take on or react to what I hear coming out of his mouth. Because I was so damaged by my codependent behavior, I lost my ability to detach. I became depressed and functioned poorly until I learned how to get back on the path of my recovery."

Relapse can happen in any stage, and it can easily take parents back to the time when addiction ran their lives. (Relapse behaviors are addressed in detail in Chapter Six.) The following actions can help parents recover from a relapse. Always remain hopeful, even if you find yourself at this stage.

Three Foundational Parenting Actions to Help You Get Back on Track

With the 5-Step Foundational Parenting Program, you can reclaim yourself and get back on track whenever there is conflict, uncertainty, fear, or an inability to find words or an answer to a question. The following Foundational Parenting actions help you take charge when you've had a misstep or lapse of any kind: stop, pause, and untangle and separate.

1. Stop What You Are Doing

Stop what you are doing, listen to your children, and concentrate on what you are witnessing in the present moment. This requires that you stop all distractions, slow down your breathing, and focus your attention on the here and now with your child. Hear what they have to say. Demonstrate with integrity that you are interested in them. As we learned in the 5 Steps of Foundational Parenting, when you pay attention and validate your child's point of view, conflicts and fights with your child will lessen. Being emotionally attuned and present without distractions always brings you back to the basics of a trusting parent-child relationship.

2. Pause Before Responding

If you need more time to respond to something your child has brought up, *pause*. Pausing is powerful. Use this simple strategy whenever you feel confused by a discussion, scared about your reaction, angry about what you see or hear, or afraid that your child's moods are controlling you and you don't want to be reactive. If you need to make a difficult decision regarding your child, take all the time you need before getting back to them with your answer. Pausing is a key tool in learning to implement your new parenting strategies. Know that you don't ever have to think of a response, a solution, or an action plan immediately. You are in charge, and you get to determine how much time you need to make a decision regarding anything affecting your parent-child relationship. You can say that you need ten minutes, a few hours, or a few days, or simply that you have to think about it and will let them know when you are ready. They may not like your refusal to respond immediately, but they will respect you more for asserting your power, whether they show it or not. Pausing is a way of being there for yourself and creating the space you need to make the best decision you can. By training yourself to pause when necessary, you also give yourself the gift of time to check in with other family members, your support network, or a treatment professional before you make a decision. *You* are in charge of your responses and actions. When you are able to consciously pause and take all the time you need, your child and his or her addictive behaviors and troubling emotions don't have control over you anymore.

3. Untangle and Separate

Untangling means choosing to protect your heart and not allowing your impulsive reactions to determine your behavior. Automatic reactions and inflexible thinking can keep parents tangled up in negative past behavior patterns. By untangling you choose to disengage with the web of addiction while still being present and available to your child. As you stop, pause, and untangle, you are able to think about what you need to do, and catch yourself before being led into a web of powerlessness. As you practice the steps, you strengthen your capacity to turn around, let go, and detach from addictive behaviors and emotions.

When you have yourself back, you see the powerlessness of addiction. Your thoughts are your thoughts. Your feelings belong to you. You will see your child as a separate person with his or her own feelings, thoughts, and challenges. Being disentangled means you can let your loved ones figure out what they need to do to thrive in their recovery journey. It means you can support your teen or young adult's journey without assuming responsibility for the work they need to do, regardless of whether they fail or succeed.

It's difficult to really separate the work of parents from their children's work, yet it is a key to rebuilding your family on a healthy foundation. Your children have their lives, and you have your life. *You* can have yourself back. Then you can turn around and see your family, hear them, and be present and empowered as parents while able to separate yourself from your loved one's addiction. All parents go through phases of uncontrollable worries and fears, especially if they think their child is using again. But your child needs you to not be

controlled by his or her moods and behaviors. Your children need you
to be strong and not react to them.

Recognize What's Behind the Addiction

Generations of parents have tried to help their child "see the light"
regarding their addiction issues, and most are met with denial, anger,
screaming matches, tears, stubbornness, and disgust. Most parents try
to break the denial with love, anger, rage, and major enabling behaviors
based on good intentions—so much so that they give themselves away
and are left with broken hearts.

Part of what keeps many parents stuck is leftover feelings of sadness
and fear due to years of chaos, turmoil, and feeling trapped by their
children's negative reactions to them, reactions that parents often
assume are a sign that their children don't care about them. It can be
hard to know whether struggling or recovering addicts care about their
relationship with their parents at all. What shows up is ugly addictive
behavior and highly reactive relationships wrapped around the past,
even from teens and young adults who are committed to recovery. As
we know, most people in recovery do want healthy, loving relationships
and many feel terrible for what they put their families through, even
though they don't voice it to their families.

Without making excuses for bad behavior, it can be helpful for
parents to realize that there is more to a child's feelings and intentions
than meets the eye. To grasp how many teens and young adults truly
feel about the way their addiction has impacted their families, read the
following responses. These statements reveal that, behind the façade
of addictive behavior and its aftermath, teens and young adults feel
remorseful and sad for the pain they have caused, but they are also
afraid of being blamed or shamed for the way their parents chose to
react to them. Learning to detach and yet not abandon their children
allows parents how to disengage from dysfunctional behavior while still
being present, loving, and kind.

"Dear Parents, I Wish You Knew"

I didn't make a conscious decision to become addicted to drugs.

I did my best and tried to be stable, but couldn't.

I have suffered so much. I feel that you only see my maladaptive behavior as an attack against you, rather than a cry for help.

I am acting out of desperation, and I need you.

You don't always know what's best for me.

I am not you. Please accept me for who I am.

My failures are my responsibility and not your fault.

I need to keep myself sober, not you.

I never wanted to hurt you with my using.

I need you to be calm and not scream at me when I mess up.

I no longer accept you pushing or using your burdens against me.

These messages express universal needs of many teenagers and young adults in recovery. Try to read them with an open mind and heart and consider what this means for your parenting. Your children want you to

- stop reacting to their feelings and problems;
- never blame them for your own unhappiness;
- listen, understand (be emotionally attuned), and respond to what they say or do;
- understand their world; and
- take charge of your own moods, and not take your feelings out on them—no child ever wants to be shamed or blamed by their parents.

Are You Ready to Take Yourself Back and Turn Around from the Addicted Behavior?

If your answer to this question is yes, then I suggest you give yourself thirty-five days, or five weeks, to begin to transform your parenting. It will take lots of dedication, practice, and patience, but it will be worth it. You can structure your learning and application of the 5 Steps in one of two ways. One option is to focus on one step for a full week and *really* work on that step for the duration of the week, then move on to the next step in the second week, and the next step in the week after that, until you've completed a full week on each step by the end of week five. Alternatively, you could take a new step each day for seven days and then repeat that pattern for thirty-five days until you've spent seven days on each step. Take whichever approach speaks to you most.

Recording your thoughts, successes, struggles, and reflections at the end of each day in a journal or notebook will help you tune in to your growth and recognize the roadblocks that interrupt your success. Following are six guidelines to help you on your way (an abbreviated version of these is in Appendix B for your easy reference):

1. Begin each day by checking in with yourself and by affirming the following statement: "I will practice rebuilding my parenting foundation today and I will work on Step _____ (whichever step you'll be working on that day). I will be mindful and catch myself when I react like I did in the past, apologize to myself and my kids, and get back on track."

2. Success is paying attention and catching yourself when you slip into old, negative reactions. When you notice old ways of coping creeping into your new journey, you will recognize that you are free and flexible to choose to get back on track and practice the step you are working on. Always keep an eye out for old behaviors that might interrupt your progress. One parent I worked with decided to work on being present for the week until we met again. Their son, Jack, lived at home and was newly sober. Every time Jack was late or nonresponsive, his dad thought he was using. His dad was scared out of his mind and felt tension all over his body. As he practiced being in the moment and not reacting to his son, he had amazing insights. His son began to confide in him more, and, for the first time in years, they began to have a real relationship. Jack felt less judged and more supported.

Dad felt fearful and worried that his son would use again, but he also learned that he could have these thoughts and anxieties without them overtaking his life. Many other parents in his support group told him that those fears rarely disappeared right away. Dad learned how to acknowledge his thoughts and fears and recognize that they weren't about the present moment, but were part of his past relationship with his son.

Notice yourself in relationship with your child as you work on the step for the week. Try to answer this question in your notebook at end of each day: "What past behaviors or reactions showed up today, and how did I deal with them?"

3. If there are challenging dilemmas with your child each day, keep reminding yourself that you don't have to respond immediately. You can pause and take all the time you need. Tell your child that you need time to think about what is being discussed. Use your support network to help process a new situation or information, if necessary. Pausing empowers parents. You don't ever have to make a split-second decision to appease your children. You have the right to pause for as long as you need to make the best decision you can.

4. Listen with an open heart to your children's point of view, without judgment. You don't have to agree; it's about listening to their view and understanding their perspective. Take nothing personally, listen openly, and make a vow not to blame and shame. Use these guidelines each day, no matter which step you are practicing.

5. At the end of each day, take a few minutes to review your interactions with your family. Be aware that your old, familiar habits have been repeated over and over for years and can easily reappear. Every time you catch yourself in old habits, look at your realization as a victory, not just for you,

but for your relationship with your children. Know that as you continue to take a stand and practice these steps, new strength will emerge and your confidence will grow and expand.

6. Share appreciation with your children about what you notice in your relationship with them. As you step forward and initiate change in your family, it's your time to soul-search and express yourself to your child from your heart. You can write a letter or note to your child along the following lines: "I want you to know how I feel as your parent and what I appreciate about you." This can happen only when you are ready to turn around from the child's addiction issues and detach from the web that has kept you unfocused up until now. Your children need to know you care about them. To help inspire you, here are some examples of appreciation letters from parents to their children:

"I am always on your side. I think you are amazing and will always be there for you. What you have been through doesn't define you. It's hard to tell you how proud I am of you for being sober. I know it's hard for you, but it is great to have you back."

"I want to trust you and am doing this more and more each day. I've been through a lot of pain with your addiction and disappearance from our family. As I get myself back together, I am beginning to have more of an open heart. I want you to know how much you mean to me and how much I love you."

"I'm trying the best I can, for you, for me, and for our family. Your success is up to you. I finally realize I can't control your drug usage and can't control your sobriety. I love you no matter what."

"I want you to be happy and content with what you choose to do with your life. All of our lives are a journey, and I'm in my own process and struggling. I always will be there for you. You are not defined by addiction and depression. You are an amazing person."

"I love you and am so proud of you. You are an amazing person. I wish you knew that my intentions are good and I am on your side."

"You have so much potential. I'm so proud of you and want to work at redoing our communication to open up a new chapter in our family. I'm trying the best I can."

"It is thrilling to be able to watch you grow up and witness you becoming a confident member of the sober community. Don't ever quit on yourself. You are precious and beautiful."

Your children need to hear how much you love them and what you are learning about your parenting to help your family grow. It is good for them to hear that you are working on being a more present parent and that you are there to support their journey in life. Model personal responsibility and accountability to them. Be patient and practice one of the steps each day until they become part of your everyday actions. You can step forward with diligence toward becoming the parent you dream of being—empowered and in charge.

Parenting Insights

- Even when your child is in recovery, know that it takes a while to really experience the transformation that can take place in your parent-child relationship.
- Too often parents promise themselves they will do things differently, and then fail to keep that promise. Be aware that success requires conscious intention and deliberate action, each and every day.

- With the 5 Steps of Foundational Parenting, you can regain yourself and get back on track whenever there is conflict, uncertainty, or fear, or when you find yourself unable to find the words to answer a question.

- Revisit the Seven Stages regularly to note where you are on your journey to taking back your parenting power. By doing so, you will be able to progress to the next stage with more flexibility, open-mindedness, and deliberate actions.

- When you pay attention and validate your child's point of view, conflicts and fights lessen. Being emotionally attuned and present without distractions is the basis of any trusting parent-child relationship.

- You and you alone get to determine how much time you need to make a decision or to respond to something in your relationship with your children. Take all the time you need to allow yourself to come up with the best response.

- Automatic reactions and inflexible thinking keep you tangled up in past negative behaviors. Untangling means you disengage while still being present and available.

- Most teenagers and young adults in recovery feel remorse and sadness about the pain they've caused you, but they don't want you to blame or shame them for your own reactions to the situation. Learn to detach from your children without abandoning them; disengage while still being present, loving, and kind.

- Tell your children how much you love them. Express how addiction has put a wedge in your relationship. They need to know that you are working on being a more present parent and that you are there to support their journey in life.

Chapter Five

Developing New Responses to Common Dilemmas

Are you tired of worrying about the right way to say things to your children? Are you fed up with anxiety from wondering how best to frame something so your children will respond to you as desired? If your answer is yes, then this chapter will be especially helpful to you. You will learn how to own your power and stop walking on eggshells. We will discuss common situations along with relevant scripts and various scenarios so you can practice and strengthen your newfound parenting power. Continue to practice so you learn how to protect your heart and avoid absorbing your children's thoughts, feelings, and difficulties. As you read through the examples, think about how you might respond to your own teen or young adult in a similar situation.

Your Children's Moods Are Not Yours

Many parents I work with express fear of their children's anger and changing moods. Their biggest fear is saying the wrong thing to them and triggering a nasty response. Parents share that they felt stuck in so many of the awkward dilemmas they faced with their children. They are at a loss as to how to respond when they disagree with what they hear from their child. Parents are also sick of the lectures that "go in one ear and out the other." I have to continuously remind parents that their children's dilemmas are not their dilemmas. When parents overinvolve themselves in their teen or young adult's problems and tell them what to do, trying to influence them with endless discussions and attempts to push them in certain directions, the children often shut down. They become quiet and unresponsive, or at times furious that their parents don't understand them. They turn their backs on their parents, and bitterness ensues. Common parental responses to such negativity include outrage, disgust, controlling behavior, obsessively trying to win arguments, or pure reciprocal bitterness.

So What Is the Parent's Role?

- Listening to your child—practice emotional attunement.
- Understanding your child's points of view (this is not about agreeing or disagreeing).
- Keeping your opinions to yourself and being nonjudgmental. (Emergencies and life-threatening situations are the exception; you need to act and be sure to get the right help immediately.) Acknowledge what you hear without judgment and without imparting your own thoughts. You could say, "Do you want my opinion?" or "Do you want help problem solving?" If your child's response is "no," you could say, "If you ever need my help, I'm here for you." You have to learn to keep your opinions to yourself—walk out of the room if you have to. When your roots are strong and you feel grounded, you will be able to stand back and observe and not get caught up in the drama of the moment. Sometimes teens and young adults want to shock their parents, and when parents don't react, the shock doesn't work.

Parents are the keepers of family values and rules. These form the bedrock and essential guide to all your parent-child interactions. When you are clear about what expectations come with living in your family, you will also be clear about the consequences of not following the family guidelines. That way, your children won't be in charge—you will.

Parents Can Listen and Keep Their Opinions to Themselves

As a parent, you really need to have a chat with yourself and decide that you can listen to and understand your teen's point of view, without interrupting and without putting your two cents in. Many adolescents and young adults roll their eyes when you interrupt them or interject your view in any way. Teenagers, especially when newly in recovery, need to vent. When this pushes your anger, panic, or fear buttons, you need to become aware of it and work hard to be able to listen without judgment.

If your teen or young adult has questions and wants you to respond but you aren't sure what to say, you can pause and not answer immediately—no matter how he or she feels or acts. You can say, "I'll need to think about that and get back to you." When they say, "I need to know now!" your response can be, "I hear that this is important to you. I need to think about what you said and I will get back to you when I'm ready." Now *you* are in charge. Your child is no longer in control of your thoughts, feelings, or actions. As you apply and practice the 5 Steps and your family heals, you will become increasingly more empowered.

Keep in mind how important pausing is. Pausing gives you time to think and check with your partner or a trusted friend who can help you sort out the decision you need to make, be it small or large. When you find yourself reacting impulsively and saying things you quickly regret, take it as a cue to pause more. Pause more frequently, and pause for longer periods. Give yourself the time and space you need. You are in charge—of what you think, feel, do, and say.

You don't need to be absorbed by your teen or young adult's thoughts, feelings, and behaviors. Your child is separate from you and can think for him or herself. Of course, all parents want to be liked, and this often influences their decisions surrounding alcohol and other drugs and their children. As you go about creating a healthier family dynamic and a stronger approach to parenting, your job is to make the best decisions you can and to live in harmony with your personal values. As your child begins to get a foothold in their recovery, they need to know that they aren't in control of your family anymore. Your true role as a parent is to love your children no matter what, and to remind them they are capable of handling what they need to handle. If they want your help, they need to ask for it.

COMMON CHALLENGES AND SUGGESTED SOLUTIONS

Following is a selection of frequently encountered problems and scenarios that have come up for parents I've worked with throughout the years. Chances are you'll be able to relate to one or more of these scenarios and therefore glean some important insight for dealing with similar situations when they arise in your parent-child relationship.

Scenario #1: Your teen or young adult screams or rages at you or slams doors. This may trigger all your buttons until you are moments away from losing it yourself. Here are some examples of how you might respond:

- Step back, become quiet, breathe, and say, "Wow, you are really mad at me. Do you want to talk about it?" If they say no, you could say, "When you are ready, I would like to listen and hear what you are so mad about. Maybe there is a way to work it out."

- Remember, your job is to listen, notice, and not absorb your child's emotions or behaviors toward you. Being present, understanding their point of view, and not reacting really can help you own yourself and your power and not absorb your children's angst.

Scenario #2: Your child tells you there is no one to hang out with at school and no one likes them. You notice tears in their eyes. At first you begin to say, "That's crazy! Lots of kids like you!" You want to defend your kid. The truth is, they don't need to be defended; they need support. Here are some ways you could respond:

- "You are crying, and seem really sad. Do you want to talk more about this? I'm here if you want me to listen to you."
- Being present, listening, and acknowledging what you hear can be a very powerful force in your child's recovery. Your role is not to work to change your children's feelings. Your role is to understand and listen.

Scenario #3: Your child is late for your agreed-upon evening curfew; how do you respond?

- When your child gets home, you meet them at the door. They apologize and share that they forgot to call. You remind them of your rules and consequences and tell them you will discuss it in the morning. Remind your child you want him or her to be safe.
- In the morning, bring it up again and remind your child you want him or her to be safe. You need to go back to family rules and institute consequences for lateness and not calling to inform you. Expect them to take responsibility for their actions, especially if they have a phone or a car, which many parents pay for. These things are a privilege, not something teenagers and young adults should assume they are entitled to. Consider taking away privileges or issuing a warning that will eventually result in a revocation of privileges if not heeded.
- Your role in this scenario is to act in accordance with your family rules and values, and to institute and carry out consequences when those rules and values are violated. By not reacting in anger the way you might have done in the past,

you continue to be in charge and able to prevent your buttons from being pushed.

Scenario #4: Your teen or young adult tells you that you are unfair and that all the other kids get to [fill in the blank]. Here's how you can respond:

- "We decided that this is how we will do this at our house. It might seem unfair to you, and I can tell you are really disappointed." Your job is to notice how they feel, acknowledge it, and listen. You don't have to change your point of view or the family rules in response to your teen or young adult's negative attitude. They can dislike what you say, but they have to realize that they live in your house. They will be able to make their own rules when they live on their own.

Scenario #5: Your child is in a bad mood, short with you, or annoyed with you on the phone or in person. You can respond like this:

- "You seem annoyed with me. Do you want to talk about it?" If your child says no, remind them that you would like to talk about it when they are ready. Your job is to acknowledge how they feel and accept what they say as their truth. Your child can feel sad, angry, lonely, or any other emotion, and you can still be okay. Your job isn't to take or fix their feelings. The gift you give your children is the acknowledgment of what you see and letting it be.

Scenario #6: "My child used again, and I'm livid!" Your teen or young adult has many excuses, starts to cry, and apologizes over and over again. They tell you they will never do it again. How do you respond?

- First, go over the contract you and your child put together at the treatment center or through the family program before he or she was discharged. If there is no discharge plan, behavior plan, or relapse plan, it's imperative that you and your child commit to creating one as soon as possible. A contract ensures that the decisions you have to make in difficult circumstances are clearly defined ahead of time.

- Be mindful not to absorb your teen or young adult's emotions, then go about determining with your partner or other support person how you want to handle this. If you are a single parent, a grandparent, or a foster parent, you may want to take a break and tell your child you will need to think about this and get back to them. Tell them you aren't ready to respond at this moment in time, but that you will get back to them by a certain time or date of your choosing. Consider reaching out to other parents in a similar situation, to your child's treatment center counselor, and/or to someone in a twelve-step fellowship. Speak to your child's other parent.

- Some parents immediately bring their child back to treatment as stipulated in the child's discharge plan. This can be an inpatient short-term program or an outpatient program.

- Some parents decide that, if the relapse is caught in the early stages, they will recontract with their child and newly outline clear expectations regarding sobriety. Many parents require random drug testing weekly. If their child refuses to be tested, it is considered the same as if they refused to be sober. In this case some parents give the child two choices: enter treatment again, or live somewhere else. Other measures to consider include immediately taking away car privileges or phone privileges, and/or withholding or reducing financial support.

Scenario #7: Your teenager or young adult is ornery when your family gets together; they're expecting everyone to fight, yell, and stress each other out like they used to. You are trying to change this, but you're meeting with a lot of resistance from your child. How do you handle this?

- Start by acknowledging the past. You can say, "I remember how hard it was when we were all together. We used to yell a lot, and not be able to all be together. We are trying to change this, and would like you to be part of this effort as our family changes."
- You are looking forward to a family meal and you want everyone to be home for it and present at the table. Your teen or young adult makes faces and asks, "Do I have to?" You can say, "We want you at our family celebration."
- Your child says, "This is so stupid. I'll come, but don't expect me to talk!" You say, "That's up to you. We want you with us." If your child is in a bad mood or sulks, just notice it and don't let it change you. You can notice what you see and move on. New dynamics evolve over time to change family patterns.

Scenario #8: Your child wants a car, wants more money, hates being at a sober-living home, or expresses some other desire or complaint. How do you respond?

- If your child is living at a sober-living home after treatment and not in your home, you need to remember why they went there to live after treatment. Most young adults who are in sober-living facilities have been through multiple rounds of treatment and need more support in maintaining their recovery to work on themselves. Parents need to remain strong, listen, understand, and not give in.
- If your child nags you for a car, you can respond, "Having a car means paying for gas and insurance. When you get a job we can talk about it." If you don't want your child to have a car, you need to tell him or her directly. If you are ambivalent, tell your child that you need to think about it. Then talk to other parents and see what they have decided and why. You always have the choice to pause and not give an answer right away, especially when you're feeling pressured by your child.

- "I hate treatment. I hate this sober-living home." Your job is to listen, acknowledge, and not back down because of pressure. Calmly and patiently remind your child why this was part of his or her recovery plan.
- With regard to money, decide how much you are willing to give your child on a weekly or monthly basis. Be clear on what you will do if your child runs out of money, and then stick to what you said. Your child's job is to figure out how to spend less, find a job, and/or budget better. Teenagers and young adults need to learn how to be independent people as they begin a new chapter in their lives.

Scenario #9: Your child issues threats such as "If you don't let me [fill in the blank], I'll use again!" What do you do?

With this kind of statement, teenagers and young adults want to make you responsible for their sobriety. You need to remember that their recovery is not your responsibility. Your job is to practice the 5 Steps to help shift you and your family onto a path of recovery, but that is all. Your children need to learn the necessary skills to deal with disappointment, fear, and pain without involving others. Your role as parent is to recognize that you can listen, hear what they say, and yet refuse to get sucked back into the vacuum addiction creates. Parents can listen to their children's points of view, but then they must make decisions based on what they think is in the best interest of the entire family. Your children don't have to like the decisions you make; you are the parent, and certain decisions are yours to make. Keep your feet on the ground, work the 5 Steps, and move toward healthy family action.

The above scenarios share one common denominator: parents of recovering addicts are just a moment away from being drawn into their children's web of addictive thinking and acting, and therefore in danger of becoming stuck the way they were during their child's active addiction. No matter the dilemma, you always have the option to pause and reflect if you are unsure about how to respond to a situation. Pausing and taking time to reflect and gather support gives you the necessary space and time to respond to the situation from a grounded place and a strong foundation. In contrast, whenever parents react immediately to a situation that is challenging and stressful, they usually tap into their old, familiar ways of coping. This means everyone's on edge and the children are in charge again.

The problems addressed above illustrate different aspects of the same basic patterns. Teenagers and young adults often want what they want immediately, without understanding the responsibility that comes with privilege. They often fight to have their way because they know their parents have backed down many times before. Their past experiences frame their approach to new experiences. The important thing to realize is that, in truth, they don't want that much power—even if they think they do. Don't give in. For your sake and for your child's sake, learn to stand your ground when faced with these challenges.

Seventeen-year-old Sam offered this poignant explanation to his parents: "I will push to get what I want. Please, don't give in! When you give in, I just try harder next time. I need you not to budge." Often when parents give in, they do so because they are afraid of their children's reactions. Parents just want peace and are willing to go against their own values to stop the rage, anger, and disappointment they see in their children. However, when parents give in to fear, they also abdicate their parenting power. Foundational Parenting teaches you how to be able to feel grounded, be nonreactive, show up as a parent, and stay true to your values by responding—not reacting—to your children.

Parenting Insights

- Your child's dilemmas are not your dilemmas. Teenagers and young adults need to take an active role in solving their own challenges, especially those created by their active addiction.
- *You are now in charge of you.* Your children no longer control your thoughts, feelings, or actions. As you practice the

5 Steps, you will become increasingly empowered and able to take charge of your family.

- Your role as a parent is to listen, understand, refrain from judgment, and be the keeper of your family's values, rules, and boundaries.
- Once teenagers or young adults enter recovery, they will need to find their place in the family again. As parents take charge differently, the whole family can take an active role in restructuring how they live together.
- Parents are always just a moment away from being drawn into their children's web of addictive thinking and behaving. Always take the opportunity to pause and reflect if you are unsure about how to respond to a situation. Pausing and taking time to reflect and gather support gives you space and time to respond and not react to the situation.
- Teenagers and young adults tend to want what they want immediately, without understanding the responsibility that comes with privilege. Each time you give in to unreasonable demands, you are making your children feel less safe. Teenagers don't want that much power, even if they think they do. They want to know that you are in charge. Don't give in.

Chapter Six

Avoiding Parenting Relapse

Not only addicts have relapses; parents of addicts can relapse too. This chapter will guide you to create your own personalized relapse plan in the event you slip back into old, unhealthy ways of interacting with your teen or young adult. By developing your own plan, you will have a benchmark from which to evaluate and interrupt old habits that may periodically show up in your parent-child relationship. A relapse plan will be invaluable in helping you become more conscious of your behavior so that you can get back on track when you detour from the 5 Steps of Foundational Parenting.

What Is Parental Codependency?

Codependency can develop in anyone who is in a relationship with someone who suffers from addiction. A codependent parent often shares some characteristics with an addict. According to the National Institute on Drug Abuse (NIDA), addicts experience mood swings related to drug use, and gradually the addict's entire personality changes to the point where all his or her thoughts and activities revolve around the addictive substance or behavior. Judgment and insight become heavily impaired, and there is an overwhelming preoccupation with substances and secretive behavior, to the detriment of all relationships and activities that were once important.[3]

Parents of addicts can be said to be "addicted" to the addict. In the same way an addict shapes his or her whole personality around one objective, parents of addicts increasingly structure their lives and sense of self around the unpredictable behaviors of their addicted child. Parents in these situations tend to make decisions based on the mood of their child rather than on what is truly healthy for them. They compromise their own value system, hoping that if they give in, their child will like them and love them to the point where the parents could make a difference in their child's addiction. As we should all know by now, this almost never happens.

Addicts base many of their thoughts and activities around the use of addictive substances or behaviors. Parents base most of their decision-making on the mood of their child. In this way the child becomes the parents' drug of choice. Parents can lose themselves in their children's reactions to them and can become overly controlling, overly involved in their daily schedules, or overly involved in speaking for their children and becoming their voice. Codependent parents allow their child's behavior, thoughts, and emotions to affect or even destroy them emotionally and, in turn, they can become obsessed with trying to control him or her.

When parents continue to support and assist teenagers or young adults in unhealthy ways and fail to let them feel the consequences of their behaviors, it inadvertently prolongs their children's pain and prevents them from growing and learning to take responsibility for their actions. Often, parents have a difficult time letting go and

---

3 A. Sarkar, "Characteristics of Drug-Dependent People" (Bogra Anti Drug Society [BADS], Bangladesh, 2004), abstract available at the National Institute on Drug Abuse (NIDA) Abstract Database, https://www.drugabuse.gov/international/abstracts/characteristics-drug-dependent-people.

detaching from their children emotionally even once they've entered recovery, because of fear, past hurts, resentment, and anger. It is critical that parents apply and practice the tools outlined in the 5 Steps of Foundational Parenting so they can learn to detach and step back. This is especially important when developing a relapse plan. Most parents slip back into old patterns of reacting regardless of whether their children are sober or experiencing a relapse.

Understanding codependency gives parents a useful perspective that can help them catch themselves when they veer off track. Step One of the Twelve Steps as practiced in twelve-step fellowships is particularly relevant to the problem of enmeshment of parents with their children. Step One drives home the idea that people are powerless over anyone else's thoughts, feelings, and behaviors. If parents try to control a child's thoughts, feelings, or behaviors, their own lives can get off track to the point of becoming unmanageable. Parents need to cultivate awareness of this tendency and learn to catch and interrupt old habits when they show up to prevent them from derailing their own recovery. When parents recognize old behaviors as soon as they show up, they are able to make a conscious choice to get back on track and stay in charge.

Does Your Child Have a Relapse Plan?

According to the Adolescent Treatment and Recovery Outcomes Review, the posttreatment home environment plays a significant role in recovery outcomes.[4] Unfortunately, a return to using—relapse—is a fairly common occurrence among adolescents.[5] Parents should be prepared and clear-eyed about the high rate of relapse. As one study puts

---

4   Richard A. Risberg and William L. White, "Adolescent Abuse Treatment: Expectations Versus Outcomes," *Student Assistance Journal* 15, no. 2 (2003): 16–20.

5   See D. Deas and S. E. Thomas, "An Overview of Controlled Studies of Adolescent Substance Abuse Treatment," *The American Journal on Addictions* 10, no. 2 (2001): 178–189; K. C. Winters, A. M. Botzet, T. Fahnhorst, and R. Koskey, "Adolescent Substance Abuse Treatment: A Review of Evidence-Based Research," in *Handbook on the Prevention and Treatment of Substance Abuse in Adolescence*, eds. C. Leukefeld, T. Gullotta, and M. S. Tindall (New York: Springer Academic, 2009), 73–96.

it, "Relapse following treatment is all too common. Some of the studies of teens who completed inpatient treatment suggest that as many as 85% report some substance use only a year after their program."[6] Most teens or young adults who complete a treatment program will leave with a plan they create with their counselors as well as parental input. The plan typically contains personal goals and steps the teen or young adult will take to support his or her recovery. Part of the plan also needs to address potential relapse, which includes not just using substances again but also engaging in any behaviors that begin the downward spiral to potential use.

It is essential that parents be a part of creating this plan, especially if their children go back home to live with them after treatment. One of the plan's main objectives is to define what both the recovering addict and the parents agree to recognize as "red flag" behaviors or situations that need to be addressed to ensure a healthy, ongoing recovery for the child and the entire family. The plan is designed to protect parents' roles by empowering them to take charge based on transparent, mutually agreed-upon guidelines that clearly dictate what steps to follow in the event of any relapse behavior.

In order to be able to follow through with the steps in a relapse plan, parents need to feel grounded and confident in their parenting foundation. Parents need their own recovery support to continue to work on separating their children's actions and emotions from their own. The six questions at the end of this chapter will guide you in creating your own parental relapse plan.

If there was no plan in place when your child left a program, it's critical that you create one as soon as possible. You need to have a written document that clearly outlines your expectations of your child once he or she gets home from treatment, as well as the concrete steps you will take if your child uses again or demonstrates using behaviors.

---

6 U.S. Department of Education, Office of Safe and Drug-Free Schools, "Recovery/Relapse Prevention in Educational Settings, For Youth with Substance Use & Co-occurring Mental Health Disorders," Report from Fall 2010 Consultative Sessions, May, 2011, https://www2. ed.gov/about/offices/list/osdfs/recoveryrpt.pdf.

Even if your child is asked to leave a program or if they leave on their own, you still need to develop a plan of expectations and consequences. All teenagers and young adults in recovery need a relapse plan to support recovery in their families. It is a cornerstone of successful recovery management for everyone involved in the recovering addict's life.

What Does Parental Relapse Mean?

Parental relapse means *reverting* to unhealthy behaviors, feelings, and actions you engaged in during your child's active addiction. Parental relapse is strongly connected to the addicted child's behaviors and actions, and parents who relapse get pulled back into the web of addictive thinking. They forget to be present with their children, become judgmental of their actions and feelings, and are reactive and ungrounded. Old behaviors are deeply ingrained and arise easily and quickly, especially when everyone is tense and trying to bring about a healthier recovering-family system. One parent shared her experience as follows: "I went home after family program and was lost. When my young adult came home, he was moody and on edge, and I just couldn't accept it. All my knowledge about addiction went out the window because I was afraid. I kept wondering how I could spend all this money on the program and he still acted the same."

The pressure of wanting your home life to be different from how it is weighs heavily on parents' hearts and minds. Without conscious and repeated practice of the 5 Steps of Foundational Parenting, familiar unhealthy habits of overreaction, worry, and hypervigilance can creep in all too easily. You need to be able to identify and recognize the triggers and traps that keep you stuck in old, repetitive actions and reactions. Find ways of reminding yourself that you can detach from your child's thoughts, feelings, and problems and that you are allowed to think and feel independently of them. Become an expert at identifying signs of relapse in yourself, as discussed in the following section.

Signs of Parental Relapse

Most studies and most of the literature on treating teenagers and young adults in recovery pay tremendous attention to relapse planning for the addict—but very little to parents of the recovering child. The following information is key to helping you identify the parental relapse behaviors that set you back. It is based on the hundreds of conversations I've had with parents in which they've shared the moments when they realized they reverted to old, unhealthy thoughts, feelings, and behaviors. I've summarized these moments in four general indicators, which I hope will provide you with some insight on how parents begin to lose themselves again to their addicted child—regardless of whether the child is using or sober—resulting in the reemergence of codependent behaviors.

1. **Living in the past or being terrified of the future.** Parents who dwell on the past, reliving memories and staying stuck in guilt, remorse, sadness, or fear have a difficult time letting go and living in the present. These parents tend to focus primarily on the unknown, fearful future for their child: "Will my child ever be able to take care of herself?" "Can my kid ever reclaim his own life apart from addiction?" In relapse thinking, parents are mentally preoccupied with, and worrying about, their child. They start to feel hopeless again as they can't seem to deal with recovery on a day-to-day, present-moment-to-present-moment basis. The focus is typically not on small steps today and taking one step at a time for these parents, but on taking a step backward and living with past fears and apprehensions.

   Let's consider Janeen as a good example of this. Her son graduated from treatment and went to recovery high school. Even though she had participated in a family program for three days in his treatment, she felt paralyzed by her history with her son. She made a decision never to trust him again, and couldn't figure out how to be with him when they were together. She nagged him about homework, she nagged him about attending his support program, and she nagged him about chores. She was unable to disengage from nagging, which put a barrier between her and her son. Learning how to detach herself from her son's addiction was very difficult. Her old ways were so ingrained that they blocked the development of new, healthy behaviors. Janeen eventually committed herself to practicing the 5 Steps of Foundational Parenting in order to get back on track. With practice, she found great success in taking her power back, staying in the present moment, and freeing herself from the addiction web.

2. **Obsessive thinking.** Parents who relapse spend excessive time worrying and are unable to focus on anyone else in the family. They are busy focusing exclusively on negative behavior. They have little or no mental space available to really listen and understand their recovering child's point of view. Unable to detach from their obsessive thoughts, these parents shut out other family members and have no time for those relationships. Randie is good example of this. Like many other parents, Randie told me that her son screamed at her all the time, accusing her of never being there with him. Her response was, "I'm with you all the time." While it is true that she was physically with him, mentally and emotionally she was still harboring and obsessing over past resentments, fears, and unresolved anger. Randie's son was furious with her. He felt lonely and desperate for her attention. She thought he was just being selfish because he couldn't see the hurt and loneliness he caused her. The blame game was her only way of relating to her son.

Finally, while he was in treatment, she began to step outside this defensive reaction loop and really worked at letting go of her son emotionally. This meant she could begin to see him as a separate person with his own thoughts, feelings, and challenges. When she was reunited with her son, she initially had to really catch herself when she automatically went back to her past, familiar feelings. When she began to use her new strategies in her relationship with him, she learned to respond instead of react, and to listen without judgment. Their relationship began to transform when she was able to be in the present moment with him and listen without reacting.

3. **Changing family rules and boundaries.** So often parents are torn between making decisions that are in line with their value system and compromising them based on fear of their child's reaction and rejection. When parents compromise their values to meet their children's wants, they get pulled back into the addiction web and hand over their power to fear and apprehension. When the teen or young adult was in active addiction, parents typically skirted rules to keep peace in the family. It is very easy to return to that place of fear, and to worry that a child will begin using again if he or she doesn't like the family rules.

   Seventeen-year-old Kim used to steal money from her parents. She would promise to change, and her parents trusted her to be true to her word. They were afraid to wield their parenting power and to enforce consequences based on the family rules and value system. Kim's parents assumed that if they just believed in their daughter enough, she would stay sober. They compromised their values out of fear of losing their child. The most troubling fear was, "What if she kills herself? We could never live with that." During family treatment, they discovered how much power they had given their daughter and they began to work on setting clear boundaries and expectations, including periodic drug testing. Kim hated the new rules, but her parents remained strong and worked as a team even though they still felt vulnerable. When Kim came home from treatment she promised to do the treatment plan, but she begged her parents to lie low on the drug testing. Even though her parents knew deep down that they should be in charge, they gave Kim power over that decision. One night they suspected she was high, but had no leverage. They were too afraid to confront their daughter—just like they had been in the past. This is a perfect example of parental relapse.

4. **Being overly helpful.** Doing more for their child than they do for themselves is a recurring theme for parents who get pulled into past behaviors. Common examples include waking children up in the morning to make sure they get to school or work, keeping the gas tank full, making sure homework is complete, and filling out college applications. During relapse thinking and acting, parents feel compelled to keep doing these things out of fear that not doing them would contribute to their child starting to use again, or to the child not achieving success in life more generally. Even once parents have become educated and fully aware that they can't cure their child's addiction and that they aren't the cause of their child's relapse, the habit of trying to save their child remains deeply ingrained and powerful. Parents have to keep telling themselves the truth—and finding ways of hearing it from others—that children need to learn from their own behaviors and face the consequences of their own actions or inactions. Recovery will never be successful if it is not pursued out of a child's own initiative and determination.

The Antidote to Parental Relapse

The 5 Steps of Foundational Parenting are designed to provide the complete antidote to parental relapse. Learn to use them as needed to bring yourself back from the brink and continue to take charge of your family. The following provides a detailed set of relapse characteristics associated with each step of Foundational Parenting. These are the factors parents should look out for as warning signs and indicators of being in danger of slipping back into old behaviors. You have the choice—always—to apply the respective step to preempt or confront your relapsed behavior. As you review these signs, take note of which ones apply to you most, and think about how you could best recognize those behaviors in the moment, and turn them around.

Step I. Practice Being Present with Your Children

Relapse signs:

- Resentment and anger regarding past challenges, addiction encounters, or legal issues.
- Emotional distance and fear of getting hurt again. You may be physically present, but always busy and unable to respond to what is going on with your full attention. You see and hear your child, but you're typically concentrating on past memories of hurt and resentment, unable to join them in the present moment.
- Inability to disconnect from technology, to the point where use of screens and devices replaces physical interaction with your children. When you obsess over multitasking, your kids feel ignored and unimportant.
- Unwillingness to see your child as being truly in recovery due to constant worry he or she will relapse, and difficulty embracing the new reality of sobriety.

Step 2. Develop Emotional Attunement with Your Children

Relapse signs:

- Intolerance of your child's ideas, feelings, and challenges. Parents slip back into judging their children harshly instead of listening and understanding their point of view in a detached way.

- Inability to listen; nagging as a way to attempt to change your child's point of view. When parents push their views, kids withdraw and become resentful. Fighting resumes or the silent treatment takes over. When parents get into the "I'm right" mode, they can no longer validate another's point of view.

- Lack of patience with your child. Active listening requires patience, pausing, and accepting periods of silence. When parents can't slow down and listen, children feel disrespected and unvalued.

- Asking questions without waiting for answers leads to communication breakdowns. To children this behavior feels judgmental and degrading. Rhetorical questions sound accusatory, and children struggle tremendously with being accused of anything, especially when what they really need is understanding and respect.

- Compulsive need to have your child open up, and an unwillingness to be satisfied with the responses given. Children often struggle in speaking to their parents, and typically use short, sometimes one-word, responses. When you find it difficult to grant your child the space to be silent and step forward when they are ready, you are slipping back into old habits. It's imperative to give newly recovering teenagers and young adults the space they need. Let them know you are available when they need you, and then back away, no matter how uncomfortable the silence may be for you. Give your children permission to be who they are. When you fail to give your children the space they need, you're telling them that their needs don't count. Emotional attunement requires parents to listen to and support their children's point of view.

Step 3. Respond to Your Children Without Judgment
Relapse signs:
- Taking children's facial expressions, emotions, and tone of voice personally. Know yourself and be able to be present without reacting to your child's expressions and tone of voice. You need to work on being non-reactive to their negative nonverbal or verbal attitudes toward you.
- Pretending to be present for your child while remaining emotionally unavailable. With built-up grief and anger from the past, this relapse sign typically manifests in facial frowns, eye rolling, body stiffness, and verbal shaming noises when you interact with your child. These behaviors are habits from the past and prevent acknowledgment of any success. They stand in the way of the 5 Steps and sabotage the emotional healing process for all parties involved.
- Repressing feelings out of fear of saying the wrong thing and pushing a child over the edge. Instead of responding to your child authentically, you shut down and revert to old habits because you're terrified any upset will lead to your child using again.

Step 4. Create Sacred Family Time
Relapse signs:
- Putting off special family events, dinners, and holidays because of your recovering child's moods.
- Canceling family plans out of fear your child will disapprove. When you do that you relinquish your role as parents and

give your children too much authority. Go ahead with your plans and simply accept it if your child doesn't show up to a family event.

- Keeping busy at the expense of sacred family time.
- Difficulty celebrating without alcohol. During a teen or young adult's treatment and early recovery, many parents decide not to drink in front of the recovering child. As recovery progresses, some parents grow resentful at being unable to drink and end up blaming the child. In this way, the initially conscious desire to be supportive by abstaining turns back into unhelpful resentment and anger.

Step 5. Clarify Values, Rules, and Boundaries

Relapse signs:

- Choosing not to enforce rules to avoid an argument or fight.
- Never completing your part of a relapse plan upon your child's release from treatment. Leaving a plan unfinished means the rules for relapse are not clearly laid out for either party, and this uncertainty will only add to existing familial stress.
- Heightened unease when your child doesn't respect family rules and values. This unease can quickly turn into relentless anger and blaming of the child. Following through on consequences becomes increasingly difficult because parents begin to slip back into the habit of taking the child's reactions personally.
- Procrastinating on developing a clear set of family rules and consequences. This avoidance keeps the family trapped in a dysfunctional system. Clarity of rules, values, and boundaries is essential in supporting recovery and strengthening your family.

Following is a summary list of the signs of parental relapse, which take both codependent parenting and relapsed parenting into consideration. Use this list to help you recognize when you are off track.

- ☐ Excessive worrying
- ☐ Feeling short-tempered
- ☐ Impatience
- ☐ Unwillingness to uphold family values and rules out of fear
- ☐ Strain on your own mental health
- ☐ Obsessive behavior
- ☐ Indecisiveness
- ☐ Reacting harshly to child's attitudes
- ☐ Controlling behavior
- ☐ Arguing over financial issues
- ☐ Walking on eggshells
- ☐ Inability to quiet your mind
- ☐ Intolerant attitude toward your children
- ☐ Inability to unplug from technology
- ☐ Yelling
- ☐ Blaming
- ☐ Feeling ashamed and detaching from friends and loved ones
- ☐ Feeling responsible for your child's recovery

Addiction and its associated behaviors never again have to rule your life!
This is the key take-away message for all parents moving forward. Wanting your home life to be healthy and wholesome already weighs heavily on your heart as a parent of a recovering child. Without diligent practice and support, familiar unhealthy habits of overreaction, worry, and hypervigilance can undermine the work you're doing to create new, healthy ways of being. It is essential for parents to catch themselves and cut off unhealthy patterns as soon as they arise if they truly desire a recovering family. Keep referring back to the 5 Steps of Foundational Parenting to detach from negativity and from overinvolvement with

your child, and to bring yourself back on track whenever a trigger knocks you off your path to recovery.

Families in recovery have to rely on strong moral support after a child's treatment. Stepping back into old ways of coping is too easy, and frustrating and unhelpful to the recovering child. Many parents are encouraged to join a twelve-step fellowship to get support for their own recovery. Twelve-step programs are a wonderful resource for many individuals, as discussed in Chapter 4. A lot of the parents I work with participate in these fellowships as a way to connect with other parents of recovering children. The support of other parents who are going through the same or similar experiences can be invaluable. However, many parents also feel they need additional support. When they are introduced to the 5 Steps of Foundational Parenting in our parenting group, they begin to feel stronger and increasingly hopeful. The 5 Steps provide them with the missing link to rebuilding their parenting foundation. They are taught to own their parenting and to detach themselves from the drama, the chaos, and the destructive behaviors of their children in active addiction. In this way, the 5 Steps of Foundational Parenting strongly complement the twelve-step fellowships.

Always remember that practicing detachment doesn't mean abandonment of your children. It means allowing yourself to think and feel independently of your children, no matter what life throws at you. Parents who apply the 5 Steps can be in charge, see their children as they are, and not absorb their children's emotions and challenges. Clear family values and boundaries are imperative in guiding parents' actions and decisions on a daily basis. As with addiction, there is no wiggle room with these rules: holding your children responsible for following your family's rules and values is imperative for their recovery.

Action Step: Create Your Own Personal Relapse Plan

In a journal or notebook, or on a separate piece of paper, answer the following questions in as much detail as possible. Take your time and reflect deeply on each topic. These prompts will guide you in determining the action steps you will take when faced with indicators of relapse behavior in yourself.

1. What behaviors have you observed in your child that you feel might trigger your old fears, anger, or worry?

2. What early-warning signs have you noticed in your own behavior that will enable you to catch yourself when you get off track? Consider reviewing the list of behaviors offered earlier in this chapter.

3. What steps can you personally take to disengage from your child's moods, thoughts, actions, or situational challenges? Review the 5 Steps of Foundational Parenting as needed.

4. Whom can you turn to for help if you find you've gone off track and need support? Make a list of these people—be they friends, family members, counselors, clergymen, therapists, or physicians—and take a proactive stance by asking people ahead of time if they would be willing to meet with you in moments of need. Keep this list in a safe and easily accessible place. Make sure you include everyone's name, email address, and cell phone number.

5. Review each of the 5 Steps of Foundational Parenting and create a list of actions that can help you get back on track when you relapse.

By developing your own personal plan, you create a benchmark to help you evaluate and interrupt old habits that may interfere with your relationship with your recovering child. The relapse plan is a vital tool for you to become more conscious of your own behavior and to regroup when you detour from the 5 Steps of Foundational Parenting.

Parenting Insights

- Parents of addicts can relapse too.
- Codependent parents share characteristics with addicts.
- An addict's mind is preoccupied with his or her addictive substance or behavior of choice. A codependent parent is similarly preoccupied with his or her child's moods, behaviors, and challenges.
- You will remain stuck in codependent behavior until you make the effort to consciously learn the strategies needed to disengage.
- Most parents slip back into old reactions to their children, regardless of whether the children are in recovery or have relapsed.
- Understand codependency so you can catch yourself when you get off track.
- Taking back your parenting power puts you in charge of what you do, what you say, and how you respond, and it's the only way to put a stop to codependent reactions to your child.
- The posttreatment home environment plays a significant role in recovery and relapse.
- Prepare for the statistically high rate of potential relapse.
- Relapse includes not just using again, but also exhibiting behaviors that begin a downward spiral toward use.
- You need to be part of relapse planning during your child's treatment, especially if the child comes home with you after treatment. Relapse plans define the red flags that both the

addict and the parents agree to address for healthy, ongoing recovery. The plan protects the parents' roles and empowers them to enforce clear, agreed-upon steps in the event of relapsed behavior.

- Parental relapse means reverting to old, unhealthy behaviors, feelings, or actions that trapped parents in an unhealthy dynamic with their addicted child. Relapsing parents get pulled back into the addiction web and forget to be present with their children. They become judgmental and highly reactive toward their child.
- You need to be able to identify the traps that keep you stuck in old, repetitive actions and reactions.
- Addiction and its associated behaviors never again have to rule your life.
- Write your own relapse plan. Invest time and care in it. Keep it in a safe and convenient place so you can refer to it whenever needed.

Chapter Seven

Reclaiming Yourself and Your Family

This chapter will provide you with an opportunity to clarify the values that guide your life, as an individual and as a member of your family. You will learn how to reintegrate these values into your family system so that your actions reflect what you say—in other words, how to "say what you mean and mean what you say" by sticking to your values and enforcing the rules you've spelled out. You will be guided to clearly define what your expectations are and what will happen if a family value or rule is broken—through the development of transparent consequences. You will further learn how to step into the freedom of detachment from addiction and addictive behaviors to once again experience joy within your family.

What Are Values?

Values guide the way we live our lives. They determine our priorities and steer our decisions, both in how we go about our day-to-day lives and how we parent our children. Clarity in our values influences how we think and the direction we take in growing and guiding our families. When parents' values and actions match up, they give themselves and their children a sense of certainty, trust, and credibility. Consistency is key; parents need to stick to their established rules, boundaries, and decisions. When parents' words and actions match, children learn from that example and are able to internalize the boundaries and expectations their parents have of their behaviors in the family.

Parenting Values Often Change with Addicted Children

Parents of addicted teenagers and young adults often change their expectations and give up what's important to them and their family in the name of "saving their kid." For many parents, saving their kids means giving in to their wishes. When parents give in, they abdicate their role as heads of the family and de facto let their children rule the home environment. Addiction puts a block between the family and consistent adherence to the family's values. Parents often reprioritize what's important, being overly focused on the addicted teen or young adult and failing to recognize how much undue power this gives their children.

In my extensive survey of recovering teens and young adults, the repeated message to parents was loud and clear: "Please hold me accountable and don't give in just because I get upset. You give me too much power!" Parents allow their children's moods, actions, and reactions to them to control too much of their lives, especially when a child is in active addiction or newly in recovery. These teens and young adults express the strong need and desire for their parents to be firm, grounded, and determined not to give in to their demands. It's not the child's role to be in control of family rules and values; parents must be in charge of their families. To "walk your walk," you need to be clear on the principles by which you live. When parents come back to what's important and hold their children responsible for their "talk and walk," the family begins to shift into a healthier dynamic.

Think of a time when you let others step over a boundary or when you yourself crossed a line with your values in the name of helping your addicted child. Remembering which violations stick out to you most can be a helpful indicator of the kind of values and principles you hold most dear. To aid you in your reflection, consider the following examples of what some other parents have shared with me, in shame and remorse, about the times when they compromised their own values.

Janet

Janet consistently put money in her daughter's bank account so she would never run low when using her debit card. Janet cosigned on the account and never wanted the account to be drained or in the red because her own credit was on the line. Her daughter constantly used up all the money, with various excuses for doing so. Most of it went to cash withdrawals to pay for drugs. Janet's fear of conflict kept her from taking charge. Her values weren't clear in her own mind, and so she was off track in her parenting. She needed to take her name off the account and set clear guidelines for her daughter with regard to how the money in the account could be used. There were no established, logical consequences for her daughter when it came to money management. Her daughter had no idea how much she should be spending, and never felt the need to get a job, since Janet provided her income. Despite Janet's belief that she had raised her daughter to be responsible with money, she had never held her daughter accountable and had strayed far from her own value system.

John and Clare

John and Clare started off as a team, but their son's addiction broke their hearts and became a wedge in their relationship. John couldn't talk directly to his son, and when Clare stepped forward and tried to set up limits and consequences, John blew up at her for being too rigid in front of their son. John kept saying, "He's twenty-one, he can figure this out." Their son still lived at home and was completely dependent on them.

Whenever he appeared sad and uncommunicative, John would give in to his demands and rarely consulted with Clare. Clare's disappointment and anger focused on John. Their relationship gradually disintegrated. Each parent secretly and separately lived in fear and worry about their son's future, but they never talked to each other about how they were feeling. With so many pent-up negative emotions between them, they lost the ability to work openly and honestly together. They gave all their power over to their addicted child. Each parent felt trapped and worn out. They had never dreamt that their loving relationship could change so drastically. What they had so highly valued in their own relationship had disintegrated when they allowed their son to drive their decisions. They needed to take back their power and relearn how to communicate with, listen to, and support each other, apart from their son.

Jake

Jake found it impossible to say no to his son. "I gave him the car whenever he wanted," he confessed, "even if he raged at me or lied about his plans. If he had failing grades in school, I called and got him off the hook in the hope he would see I was on his side." Jake lived in terror of the possibility that his son might kill himself if he stood up to him. His values of respect, taking responsibility for one's schoolwork, and accountability went ignored in favor of keeping the peace. Unfortunately, this gave his son all the power in the family and let him dictate his own rules. Even without outward conflict, their family was fractured.

I hear stories like these over and over again, both from parents whose children are in active addiction and from those whose children are in recovery. Parents violate their own boundaries to get on their children's good sides and mistakenly think they are helping them by doing so. Everyone needs to be on the same page when it comes to family expectations, rules, and boundaries, and parents, working together, need to be the ones who establish and enforce these for the family.

Clarity about your parenting and family values will help you support your children and provide an example of how to act and make decisions. When you are clear about boundaries and rules in your family, your children will know when they cross the line and what natural or logical consequences they should expect to help them get back on track.

Action Step:

As a first step, articulate what's important to you as a parent. What are your values? In your journal or notebook, write down what matters to you most in each of the following areas. If you completed the action step in Chapter 3, refer back to the answers you gave then, and try to go even deeper this time.

Area of Life	My Values and Expectations
Chores	
Schoolwork	
Mealtime	
Family time	
Holidays	
Money	
Feelings	
Friendships	
Kindness	
Helping	
Spirituality	
Communication	
Independence	
Using addictive substances/engaging in addictive behaviors	

Types of Consequences: Natural and Logical

There are two types of consequences: *natural* and *logical*.

Natural consequences occur as a result of a particular behavior. Examples include receiving a failing grade because a project was not handed in, not having money for something because it wasn't budgeted for carefully, or having a license revoked for not paying a ticket. With addicted and recovering children, it is imperative to let natural consequences occur without interfering with them. Often parents hire attorneys, perform the necessary interactions, and become their children's advocates in an effort ensure that they have a clean slate. As a result, these children don't learn the natural consequences of their own actions, and don't get the opportunity to take responsibility for them. Such consequences include legal issues such as DUI charges and speeding tickets, graduation problems at school, and overdrafts on checking accounts.

How can children learn to be responsible if a parent is always stepping in to save them from experiencing the consequences of their actions? Being sober and in recovery is a special challenge, and one that your children can learn to master if you let them figure out how to lead a life with integrity, boundaries, and values. Help your teen or young adult by stepping back and allowing him or her to step forward to deal with his or her own mistakes. You can offer support, but don't take responsibility for the choices your children have made.

The other types of consequences are logical. Logical consequences do require intervention from a parent. In order to have suitable, proportionate, and logical consequences for your children when they violate a rule, it is essential to craft clear and explicit expectations for your child when he or she returns from a treatment program, comes home to visit, or comes home to live. It is even more important to have such explicit expectations in place if your child relapses or refuses treatment. Creating a list of rules and expectations for your child is a foundational step in taking your family back from addiction. Clear values, rules, and consequences will be your saving grace when you are confronted by difficult situations. Many parents need help in figuring out appropriate consequences for difficult situations, and the following section will guide you in developing a plan that will work for you.

Examples of Logical Consequences in Difficult Situations

The following stories illustrate the way some parents dealt with various scenarios that came up with their child during and after treatment. As you read, pay attention to the themes that run through these examples.

John and Nancy

John and Nancy are parents of a twenty-two-year-old son who hated treatment and begged to come home. He promised he would never use again and wanted another chance. His treatment was part of the court-ordered natural consequence that resulted from his driving while intoxicated for the third time. In the past, his parents had gotten him off the hook by hiring expensive attorneys and minimizing his consequences. This time, John and Nancy decided they had had enough and were tired of all the drama and their son's refusal to take responsibility for his actions. They knew if he left treatment early, he could possibly serve jail time and his graduation from college would be delayed. Both parents put in a tremendous amount of effort to create a plan to stop fighting his battles for him so he could take responsibility for his behavior. They both needed to agree and have clarity to avoid being confused emotionally when their son complained to them. They could no longer afford to be controlled by his emotions. They needed to be empowered and live by their own expectations, not his. Together, they created the following four rules with *no room* for negotiation:

1. Their son needed to finish treatment and follow through with their recommendations. If this wasn't accomplished, he would have to find his own place to live.
2. Their son needed to be in contact with a family attorney and court regarding his DUI. John and Nancy would step

aside and let him figure out where to take it from there. They would counsel him if he needed advice, but they would not do any of the work for him.

3. When home on visits, use of substances of any kind would not be tolerated. If they suspected use or witnessed rage-filled, disrespectful behavior, their son would have to leave.

4. Because of the third DUI, he would have no access to a car. If he carried through with their recommendations and asked for their help, they would help him figure out his transportation needs.

Scott

Scott couldn't stand all the bickering with his seventeen-year-old daughter, and he gave in to her all the time. He couldn't say no or enforce limits on behaviors such as missed curfews, unfinished homework, or lackluster school attendance. His daughter had all the control in the family because Scott feared her moods. She was still sober after four months of treatment, but her temper was ornery. Scott thought he was protecting her recovery by disengaging as a parent. He came to the 5-Step Foundational Parenting group and started to see how his approach was counterproductive. What he needed to do was set clear expectations and detach from his daughter's moods. The more untangled he became, the better he could take a stand and clarify his rules and expectations with her. He asked other parents how they handled their children's bickering, and received invaluable input and helpful perspectives. He heard other parents articulate how when they were clear about expectations and consequences, they felt more in control and less defensive. The more they followed through on what they said they would do, the more their children respected them and stayed on track. Scott put together a plan for his family's values and boundaries, and then he asked for some suggestions from his daughter. For the first time she felt heard by him, and he wasn't defensive, reactive, or withdrawn. His daughter knew he meant business, and she was able to give her opinion on curfews, accountability for her responsibilities, and car expenses.

Lincoln

Twenty-seven-year-old Lincoln had just left his eighth treatment and was now in a sober-living situation. His parents were worn out and drained from all the fear and drama surrounding their son. After six months in sober living, he was given a pass to fly home for a long weekend. Before that could happen, the sober-living home contacted his parents and helped them formulate a plan, together with Lincoln and his counselor, for their expectations about the weekend. First on the list of expectations was attendance at a twelve-step meeting at least once a day. He also had to report where he would be when he left his parents' home. Last, he had to accept that he could not hang out with his old using buddies. If Lincoln relapsed while at home, his parents would ask him to leave or take him back to treatment, sober living, or detox. Lincoln requested at their meeting that, if he used again, they take him back to detox, even if he was defensive.

In the past, Lincoln's parents had never followed through with their consequences and would make new rules instead so as not to have to hold him accountable for his actions. They weren't ready to carry through with what they had said they would do while their son was in the grip of his addiction. Now, they'd finally had enough and had learned how not to become absorbed by their son's moods, demands, or challenges. They now had strategies with which to take charge and shift their family dynamics toward recovery.

One day Lincoln came home and refused to account for where he was going to take the car. His parents knew that their son's refusal to let them know where he was going was out of line and a possible setup for using again. They worked as a team and took the car keys away, refusing to give them to him for the remainder of his visit. This was the first time Lincoln had witnessed his parents working as a team and taking charge. Without the car at his disposal, Lincoln had to ask friends to come over to his parents' house. Lincoln's moodiness with his parents lessened when he knew he wasn't the boss of the house anymore.

What these three stories have in common is that all the parents began their journey toward recovery being controlled by fear, and by their children's moods and challenges. When they became clear about their expectations in their home and followed through on them, the family dynamic shifted. Their children didn't have to like it, but they did learn that they needed to abide by the rules. In all three cases the parents became empowered to set clear limits and stick to them.

Creating a Home Contract That Works with a Treatment Exit Plan

The following action step guides you through developing a posttreatment plan in case of relapse, both for you and for your recovering child. You will naturally figure out which parts of the contract are set in stone and which parts leave room for discussion and negotiation. Regardless of their age, when children feel heard by their parents, they are far more likely to be compliant and work with them. In fact, if you ask children what rules they think they should be following, they are usually stricter and more severe in their own idea of consequences than their parents are.

A "do-it-or-else" attitude rarely works with teens or young adults. Sometimes, your children will refuse to participate. Even in treatment programs, when it's time to think about leaving and planning, some children are sure the rules don't apply to them, and they respond with a negative, noncompliant attitude. Parents need to let their children know that their choice not to participate doesn't influence what their parents have put together. Parents need to make it clear that they intend to follow whatever guidelines they outline in their contract or letter. They also need to remind their children that if they don't like something in the contract, it still needs to be followed. Forfeiting the opportunity to help design it does not mean forfeiting the responsibility to abide by its rules. It is essential that you don't allow yourself to be controlled by your uncooperative child. You must be grounded, calm, nonreactive, and clear in your intentions.

Action Step: Create a Contract in Seven Steps

1. Whether you are the sole parent or part of a parenting team, it's imperative that you define your family's core values first. You need to take time to really think about what's important to you before presenting these terms to your child. Use the list of values you created in response to the action step on page 111.

2. Ask everyone in your family to get together to go over your core family values. Present your list to them and ask what else they might add. Ask if they are in agreement with what you came up with. If not, listen to their reasons and assure them you will take their ideas into consideration as you keep developing the family core-values list. Your job is to keep working on a master list, with everyone's ideas taken into consideration.

3. Identify problem areas in your day-to-day relationship with your children. Consider such issues as disrespectful communication, unresolved legal issues such as speeding tickets or DUI charges, overdrafts on checking accounts, unpaid credit card bills, or money issues in general, lapses in sobriety, poor grades, poor school attendance, or the inability to maintain a job.

4. Make a list of changes you expect with regard to each of these problem areas. Then come up with a set of natural and logical consequences for each. Consider the following examples:
   - If your child was discharged from a treatment program and is taking medications for co-occurring mental health challenges, his role upon discharge is to take his medications and work with a psychiatrist or

therapist in his community. You expect your child to follow through with treatment recommendations, and you hold him accountable for taking his medication and meeting regularly with his therapist. The logical consequences for not following through, especially if your child still lives at home, could be to deny certain privileges such as having access to a car, using a phone, going out with friends, or anything else you think would be helpful. When your child does follow through, he will earn the privilege of your trust. When he follows through, you can reward him by reinstating some of his privileges.

- Your child used all of her savings and checking account money and went into overdraft. She maxed out on credit cards to pay for her substance of choice and now has huge debts on her shoulders. Your expectations clearly state that she will get a job and figure out how to pay everyone back and pay off every credit card. Possible consequences if she doesn't find a job and figure out how to pay everyone or every card might include no extra spending money from parents (a logical consequence), continued debt (a natural consequence), and a poor credit rating (a natural consequence). Privileges will resume when she finds a job and uses her income to pay back her debt. You can work out a deal with your child on how much she will need to pay back by a certain time, and be available to consult with her to help her figure out how to pay off the remaining debt. Remember, however, that it's not your job to do the work, and that your child must pay off the debt herself.

5. Keep adding to the list in Step 4 until you have a total of five areas that you and your child will be working on.

6. Create a written contract, either by hand or on the computer, that explicitly states each of the items you identified in the above steps.

7. Set a date, perhaps thirty or sixty days from the date of the contract, when you will revisit the agreement to make sure it is on track and to renegotiate some of its terms if necessary. This provides an opportunity to deal with your child's follow-through, or lack thereof, with the initial contract.

The contract you've drawn up can also be part of a treatment-exit plan. The key is that you, the parent, must reinforce what's important in your family and stay true to your values. This contract can be a win-win for both you and your child, if you work together.

How to Hold Teens or Young Adults Accountable to the Plan

Your role as a parent and as the keeper of your family contract is paramount to shifting your family into a healthy dynamic. This means *you* are in charge of holding everyone accountable to live by your family's values and rules. You need to take the time to pay attention to your children's day-to-day lives and notice when they are on track. Paying attention to their follow-through, effort, and recovery is essential in reestablishing trust on both sides.

Some families have family meetings, perhaps once a week during dinner, to check in and go over positives for the week as well as areas that need work.

Be prepared for the possibility that your child will balk at accountability. Accountability often goes out the window with addiction, and no matter how parents try to hold their addicted teen or young adult accountable, they may get beaten down by their child's noncompliance and disrespect. If this happens, your job is to slow down, pay attention to your children, and make sure you use logical consequences to help them get back on track. There are no free rides when you live in a recovery family.

What If My Child Doesn't Live at Home?

Young adults might have their own apartment or live with roommates. Some are in extended sober-living situations and may feel unsure about where they will live when they leave that program. Others need a place to stay because of limited funds, lack of work, or difficulty in school. Again, there are no free rides for anyone, whether they are in recovery or still in active addiction. Therefore, parents of young adults need to determine what role they will take in financial situations, including whether or not they will chip in for their children's rent, car payments, insurance premiums, and general living expenses. Parents need to consider their core values and make sure that whatever they decide to do is in alignment with those values. Consider whether the role you play is keeping your child dependent or is helping him or her to become independent and live within his or her own income.

Anticipate the many occasions when your family will gather for celebrations, dinners, visits in or out of town, and vacations. When meeting up with your child in these scenarios, you need clarity on your expectations, especially since such events may have been very difficult in the past. Two of the most important questions for you to answer are "What will you do if your recovering child's mood or behavior makes the time together difficult and uncomfortable or they relapse into addiction?" and "How will you make your expectations clear to them before you get together?"

If your young adult is in a good place—that is, actively working on his or her recovery and trying to turn his or her life around—he or she might be more open to following your rules and expectations. However, if he or she is defensive and making interacting difficult, you need to work extra hard on the 5 Steps of Foundational Parenting to avoid absorbing their reactions to you.

Holding Your Child Accountable

Most parents need a lot of practice, especially in the beginning of recovery, to self-monitor their emotional ups and downs. To break out of deeply ingrained, long-established methods of reacting to their children in unhealthy ways requires diligent practice, over and over again. Conscious intention and frequent check-ins (with yourself, with your partner or a friend, or perhaps through a support group) can help you cultivate an increasingly positive way of relating to your children.

The 5 Steps of Foundational Parenting help you take charge, be available for your children, and own yourself again. The 5 Steps teach you to pause, stop, and untangle from your enmeshment with them. When you can do this consciously, repeatedly, you will eventually reach a point when you are able to make wise decisions in almost any situation.

If you ever get stuck or experience a relapse into overinvolvement, controlling behavior, fear, and giving in, you can catch yourself and get back to your core values by turning to the 5 Steps. You will not be driven by your reactions to your children. You will respond according to your values and expectations and work on never deviating from them again. Your children will no longer be in charge of you. Your core values will dictate how your family operates, and you will be in charge of holding everyone accountable to the rules and values that matter to you most.

Parenting Insights

- When your values and actions match up, it creates a sense of certainty and trust between you and your children.
- Being clear on your parenting values influences your thinking, your decision-making, and the direction you take in your family.
- Addiction often blocks a family's ability to consistently adhere to the family's values. Parents compromise on what matters most because they're overly focused on the addicted person.
- Putting your values in writing helps you maintain your focus on what's important to you.
- Allow your child to experience the natural consequences of their actions without interfering. Help your teens or young

adults take responsibility for their actions by stepping back and letting them step forward to fix the messes they create.

- You can be present for and supportive of your children, but you should not do your children's work for them.

- Clearly defined values and rules and explicitly stated consequences are your saving grace in difficult situations. Use them as a guide to keep you on your path in weak moments.

- Sometimes a child will refuse to participate in creating a family contract, even when asked for an opinion. Let your children know that their choice not to participate in building a contract doesn't mean they don't have to abide by its terms.

- Don't allow yourself to be controlled by your uncooperative child.

- Create a contract with your newly sober child and use it as a guideline for what values and rules you need to adhere to as a family. Create this contract even if your child is still in active addiction and refuses to get help. The key is that you be in charge of your expectations with regard to every member of your family.

- It is your job as the parent to hold everyone accountable to live by your family values and rules. Take time and pay attention to your children's day-to-day lives and notice when they are on track and doing the right things.

- Practice the 5 Steps of Foundational Parenting to help you feel grounded, in charge, responsive, values-driven, and emotionally attuned to your children. When you apply the 5 Steps your children will feel heard, their ideas will be taken into consideration, and you will be in charge of your family.

Conclusion

Teens and young adults who are new in recovery and committed to sobriety hold valuable insights that they, unfortunately, rarely share with their parents. The candid wisdom they've shared with me through my surveys and years of individual sessions can help you better understand your recovering child's needs on a personal, heartfelt level. Allow yourself to really hear what they are expressing in the following summary of their responses. If you let their words sink in, you will find in them all the wisdom you need to step up and take back your parenting power, be in charge of your family, and support your child's recovery.

As we discussed at the beginning of this book, most children desire a strong, loving, healthy relationship with their parents. But parents often feel pushed away by their children's defensiveness, which in turn is the result of their own guilt, shame, and remorse. While children's explicit actions and words often make it seem like they don't care, in truth they really do care—a lot. Most parents of recovering teens and young adults have a hard time recognizing this because of the difficult path they have been on with their children. Please stay open to the reality that children do need their parents—and that includes you.

Most recovering teens and young adults feel tremendous remorse for what they have put their parents through. It is imperative for parents to understand the disease of addiction and be patient as their children slowly unveil their true selves and, hopefully, recover.

"What difficulties have you encountered in your relationship with your parents?"

- I have difficulty with honest communication and setting respectful boundaries.
- We are way too enmeshed with each other.
- It's difficult to get my parents' support because I have to stay completely sober.
- I don't feel safe visiting my parents and talking about my trauma. They always butt in on conversations and don't listen.
- It's difficult to communicate my underlying emotional issues with them.
- Whenever I go home, my parents preach to me or try to make me believe their views on everything.
- My parents think they know what's best for me and prefer to make my decisions for me. They ignore me and never ask my opinion.
- I owe my parents thousands of dollars that I stole from them while I was addicted. They have no idea how much I ripped them off. I need to pay them back to work on my honesty and remorse.

"What do you wish your parents knew about you?"

- I wish they knew that I really did my best and tried to be stable, but couldn't. I also wish they recognized how much I have suffered with my addiction.
- Sometimes I feel really sad that my parents only see my maladaptive behavior as an attack against them, rather than as a cry for help or an act of desperation.

- I am an adult, and you can't keep making my decisions for me. You don't always know what's best for me without discussing my ideas first.
- I don't want to hurt them like I have in the past ever again.
- I am trapped in a vicious cycle. As the family's black sheep, I've given up trying to appear good in their eyes. No matter how much I do right or how much I succeed, I am always under the microscope for my wrongdoings.
- My parents' lack of trust has forced me to stop caring about trying to do things the right way. Since spending time away from them, I have rediscovered who I am. I now know I am a good person, and I hope one day they will see that, too.
- I love and miss my parents so much.
- Please accept me for who I am and realize I am not you.
- I'm trying very hard to change. I love myself and I love my family.
- I'm a kind-hearted person and my emotions are valid. I can keep myself sober, not you.

"What do you appreciate about your parents?"

- I appreciate how loving they are to me, even when I don't respond to them.
- I appreciate their willingness to spend their hard-earned money on my treatment.
- I appreciate that they never gave up on me.
- I appreciate that my mother loves and supports me, no matter what I do.
- I appreciate that my parents only want the best for me.
- I appreciate my parents because they are genuinely good people. They are selfless in supporting me.
- I appreciate the fact that my parents have tried their best.
- I appreciate my parents' unconditional love and support, and their understanding that addiction doesn't happen in a

bubble. My parents' willingness to take part in my recovery was awesome and so helpful.

- I appreciate my dad.
- I appreciate their undying support in every aspect of my life and their unconditional love.

"What wise words can you share with parents regarding your journey in addiction?"

- I am fragile in my early recovery after my overdose. I have a bad memory. Please help me understand why you yell instead of talking to me. I need you to be patient and kind with me as we go forward. Please stop hurting me.
- I wonder why you keep trying in our relationship, especially since I am so headstrong. I'm the one who sabotages our relationship.
- I want my parents to know that I forgive them, and I want to know whether they forgive me.
- I want you to know that I can't do this alone. I need you to be on my side.
- I'm an adult on paper, but inside I am a kid. Why don't my parents ever try to change and be there for me?
- I love my parents, even if I don't always show it.
- If I make a mistake, please let me live with the consequences of what I do.
- I need my parents to show me that they care and love me. When they don't do that, it hurts me more than anything. I am changing, and I want them to tell me what I can do to be a better child. I want a relationship with my parents.
- We have feelings that mean a lot to us. Please listen and understand us.
- My spirit can be easily shattered. Being a child of divorce is an unwanted admittance into a club that you would never wish on any kid. Never put your kids in the middle of their parents' divorce or fighting.

- I love my parents more than anything, and I feel so bad for what I put them through.
- Please give me another chance and support me as I change in sobriety.

These powerful messages are a testament to the need for a loving, caring, supportive relationship between recovering children and their parents. These teens and young adults love their parents and want them on their side. They feel guilt and remorse for what they put them through in their active addiction. Each message is heartfelt and representative of the responses from the 300 teens and young adults who took this survey. Teens and young adults want their parents to be present with them and to show how much they care. They want their parents to be emotionally attuned to them, to remain nonreactive to what they witness and hear, and to hold them accountable for following family rules and expectations. These children need their parents to engage with the 5 Steps of Foundational Parenting. Parents need these steps to help them disengage from the web of addiction, whether their children are still in active addiction or are in the early stages of recovery.

Always remember that you can make a difference in your family. The 5 Steps of Foundational Parenting are designed to teach you how to detach emotionally from your child's addiction challenges and to take back your parenting power. When you understand the effects of addiction on the whole family, and especially on your role as a parent, you will be able to understand more completely how you stopped growing and became stuck. The 5 Steps give you the tools you need to turn your parenting and your family around and take charge with renewed health and a hopeful spirit.

As you move forward, remember that parents can also relapse. You need a plan in place that can help you realize when you fall off track. Your children also need a plan to identify behaviors that could lead them into relapse, so that these behaviors can be avoided. Don't underestimate the importance of defining your family's core values and expectations; this is imperative as you move forward on your recovery journey. Clear values, rules, and consequences will be your saving grace when you are confronted with difficult situations. In weak moments, you will be able to refer to your written list of values as a guide to keep you and your children safely on your path to recovery. Clarifying and articulating your parenting values will influence your thinking, your decision-making, and the direction you take in your family.

Remember what teens and young adults in recovery need from their parents: join them as they are, be present for them, listen to their opinions, treat them with respect, and respond to their needs. Stay firm on what you believe and do not give your children power over you. They want to know that when they cross the line, you will help them back on the path by allowing natural consequences to occur and by enforcing logical consequences for their own benefit. Last, and most importantly, your children want you in their lives again. Allow the 5 Steps of Foundational Parenting to guide you as you go forward in your parenting and recovery journey. Addiction and its associated behaviors never have to rule your life again.

Appendix A

Overview of the 5-Step Foundational Parenting Program

Step 1. Practice being present with your children. Being present helps you step back from worries and anxieties. Teens and young adults need you to pause, turn around, and be present. You can be in charge of your own thoughts, feelings, and actions. You can have worries and feelings, and still be present for your family. Addiction doesn't have to rob you of your everyday emotions, time, energy, or mental space. You *can* stop, pause, and focus on the present moment, giving yourself the freedom to connect with your family members. This step calls you back from worries and anxieties in your own life.

Step 2. Develop emotional attunement with your children. Witness your children as they are and understand their point of view. It's not your job to take on their emotions, thoughts, or problems. This step helps you understand another point of view; it's not about agreeing or disagreeing. Your role is to create sacred space to understand what your children are thinking and feeling. Your children want you to listen to their feelings and thoughts and validate what you hear. Your role is to see them as they are, *not* as you wish they would be. Put aside your feelings and thoughts and join your children as they are to really see them.

Step 3. Respond to your children without judgment. Witness and observe your children without judgment. Find the time to be available to respond to your children's needs by communicating, listening, and paying attention. As you begin to be more present, more attuned, and less reactive, your children will become more trusting of you because they observe that your actions, words, and intentions match. You can learn to show up, take charge, listen, be nonjudgmental, and stop yourself from leaping to conclusions before you understand your children's point of view.

Step 4. Create sacred family time. The "child spirit" can be part of everyone's day-to-day life. Be present and connect with your children with lightness, gentleness, and compassion. Create sacred space and time and find new family rituals and celebrations. Your children want you to help rekindle the "child spirit" in your family, no matter what is taking place. This step is critical for reestablishing familial trust. Family celebrations and rituals can help heal your relationships.

Step 5. Clarify values, rules, and boundaries. No matter how old your children are, they need to know the rules and what consequences will occur if the rules are broken. When you are able to be in the present moment, you can reinforce the limits and values in your family. Clarify your values and live within those values. Your children need you to be in charge of them in loving, caring ways while enforcing the rules and setting clear boundaries. As you begin to rebuild your foundation, it is imperative to redefine the important values by which members of your family are expected to live. Over time, your choice to remain firm on values, boundaries, and rules will reestablish trust in your family.

Appendix B

Thirty-Five Days to Transform Your Parenting

Take the next thirty-five days, or five weeks, to begin to transform your parenting. You can focus on one step for a full week, then move on to the next step in the second week, and the next step in the week after that, until you've completed a full week on each step by the end of week five; or, you can take a new step each day for seven days and then repeat that pattern for thirty-five days until you've spent seven days on each step. For either of these approaches, do the following every day:

1. Each morning, affirm this statement: "Today, I will practice rebuilding my foundation and work on Step _____ (whichever step you'll be working on that day). I will catch myself when I automatically react like I did in the past, apologize to myself and my kids, and get back on track."

2. Throughout the day, be conscious of the step you are working on. Keep an eye out for old behaviors in yourself that might interrupt your new strength. Acknowledge when you are able to sidestep old behaviors.

3. If you face a challenging dilemma with your child, remember that you don't have to respond immediately. Pause and take all the time you need. Be clear with your child that you need to take time to think about what is being discussed. Call on your support network, if necessary, to help process information. You have the right to pause to make the best decision you can.

4. Listen with an open heart to your children's point of view without judgment. You don't have to agree; it's about listening to their view and understanding their perspective. Don't take anything personally; listen openly, and make a vow not to blame or shame your child for what they are expressing. Follow this guideline no matter which step you are practicing.

5. At the end of each day, take a few minutes to review your interactions with your family. Take note of any old, familiar habits that may have reappeared. You can work on correcting these habits the next day. Also take note of any victories. You can work on creating more of these in the days to come.

Each week during the thirty-five-day period, check in with yourself on how your new approach is working. Do you need to make some adjustments? Do you need to put more effort into a particular step? Which steps require less effort? Also, check in with your child and listen to what he or she has to say with regard to your parent-child relationship and how things are going in your family.

When you begin to step forward and initiate changes in your family, you can spend some time soul-searching to prepare to write a letter to your child from your heart. (Chapter 4 can help you frame this letter.) The time to write this letter is up to you. Perhaps you want to do it at the end of thirty-five days, or even sooner.

Resources

Al-Anon

A twelve-step support group offering meetings where friends and family members of addicts share their experiences and learn how to apply the principles of the Al-Anon program to their individual situations. Younger family members and friends can also attend Alateen meetings. You can learn that you are not alone in the problems you face, and that you have choices that lead to greater peace of mind, whether the addict continues to use or not.

www.al-anon.org

Families Anonymous

A twelve-step fellowship for families and friends who have known the feeling of desperation concerning the destructive behavior of someone close to them, whether caused by addiction or by related behavioral problems. Any concerned person is encouraged to attend meetings, even if there is only the suspicion of a problem.

www.familiesanonymous.org

Nar-Anon

A worldwide twelve-step fellowship for those affected by someone else's addiction. Attend meetings to receive help from group members and listen to others share their experience, strength, and hope.

www.nar-anon.org

Narcotics Anonymous

1 (818) 773-9999

Provides literature and information on recovery and local twelve-step meetings.

www.na.org

National Alliance on Mental Illness (NAMI)
The largest grassroots mental health organization dedicated to building better lives for the millions of Americans affected by mental illness.
www.nami.org

National Association for Children of Alcoholics (NACoA)
1 (888) 554-COAS or 1 (888) 554-2627
NACoA is the national nonprofit organization working on behalf of children of alcoholic- and drug-dependent parents. The website offers important information for parents and a special link for kids.
www.nacoa.org

National Council on Alcoholism and Drug Dependence (NCADD)
NCADD and its Affiliate Network is a voluntary health organization dedicated to fighting the Nation's number-one health problem—alcoholism, drug addiction, and the devastating consequences of alcohol and other drugs on individuals, families, and communities. A great resource for parents.
www.ncadd.org

National Institute on Drug Abuse (NIDA)
Publishes the latest science-based information about the health effects and consequences of addiction and offers resources on how to talk with kids about the impact of drug use on health.
www.drugabuse.gov

Partnership for Drug-Free Kids
Parents' toll-free helpline: 1 (855) DRUGFREE or 1 (855) 378-4373
Monday to Friday, 10:00 a.m. to 6:00 p.m. EST
You can talk to other parents and experts about drug and alcohol addiction, treatment, and recovery.
www.drugfree.org

The Substance Abuse and Mental Health Services Administration (SAMHSA)
The agency within the U.S. Department of Health and Human Services that leads public health efforts on advancing the behavioral health of the nation. SAMHSA's mission is to reduce the impact of substance abuse and mental illness on America's communities.
www.samhsa.gov

Recommended Reading

Brown, Brené, *The Gifts of Imperfection: Let Go of Who You Think You're Supposed to Be and Embrace Who You Are*, Center City, MN: Hazelden, 2010.

Brown, Stephanie Brown, *The Family Recovery Guide: A Map for Healthy Growth*, Oakland, CA: New Harbinger, 2000.

Covey, Sean, *The 7 Habits of Highly Effective Teens*, New York: Touchstone, 2014.

Foote, Jeffrey, Carrie Wilkens, Nicole Kosanke, and Stephanie Higgs, *Beyond Addiction: How Science and Kindness Help People*, New York: Scribner, 2014.

Hayes, Steven, C., *Get Out of Your Mind and Into Your Life: The New Acceptance and Commitment Therapy*, Oakland, CA: New Harbinger, 2005.

Lee, Joseph, *Recovering My Kid: Parenting Young Adults in Treatment and Beyond*, Center City, MN: Hazelden, 2012.

Mogel, Wendy, *The Blessing of a Skinned Knee: Using Jewish Teachings to Raise Self-Reliant Children*, New York: Penguin, 2001.

Nakken, Craig, *The Addictive Personality: Understanding the Addictive Process and Compulsive Behavior*, Center City, MN: Hazelden, 1996.

Siegel, Daniel J., *Brainstorm: The Power and Purpose of the Teenage Brain*, New York: Tarcher/Penguin, 2015.

Siegel, Daniel, J. and Mary Hartzell, *Parenting from the Inside Out: How a Deeper Self-Understanding Can Help You Raise Children Who Thrive*, 10th Anniversary Edition, New York: Tarcher/Penguin, 2013.

Wegscheider-Cruse, Sharon, and Joseph Cruse, *Understanding Codependency: The Science Behind It and How to Break the Cycle*, Updated and Expanded Edition, Deerfield Beach, FL: HCI, 2012.

Wolf, Anthony E., *Get Out of My Life, but First Could You Drive Me and Cheryl to the Mall: A Guide to the New Teenager*, New York: Farrar, Straus and Giroux, 2002.